CONVERTING
OLD BUILDINGS

Into New Homes

CONVERTING OLD BUILDINGS

Into New Homes

**Barrie Davies with Nigel Begg
Photography by Nigel Rigden**

CROWOOD

First published in 2004 by
The Crowood Press Ltd
Ramsbury, Marlborough
Wiltshire SN8 2HR

www.crowood.com

Paperback edition 2010

British Library Cataloguing-in-Publication Data
A catalogue record for this book is available from the British Library.

ISBN 978 1 84797 196 8

Disclaimer
At the time of going to print the information in this book is true and complete to the best of our knowledge. All recommendations are made without any guarantee on the part of the publisher, who also disclaims any liability incurred in connection with the use of this data, or specific details.

Acknowledgements
The authors would like to thank the following in particular for their invaluable help with this book: The Royal Institute of British Architects; Harry Montresor and Sarah Rogers; Andy Hooker and Anna Botterell; English Heritage, National Monuments Records; Martin and Lynne Whitfield; Hugo and Kate Wyhowski; Ed Seymour and Marianne Taylor-Seymour; The Bat Conservation Trust; The Joint Contracts Tribunal Ltd; The National Building Specification; HMSO; and South Somerset District Council.

Typeset by Jean Cussons Typesetting, Diss, Norfolk

Printed and bound in Malaysia by Times Offset (M) Sdn. Bhd.

Contents

Introduction

Converting old and dilapidated buildings is not for the faint-hearted. It is unlike building a new house on a virgin plot with new materials. It is not so easy to create your dream home from a ruin or an old cow barn and it takes a lot of imagination and perseverance to achieve what you want. In addition, some of the buildings chosen may be difficult to convert into usable spaces and your ingenuity will be stretched to the limit.

It is a challenge in which you will have to confront all sorts of issues such as defective structures and repairs, wood rot, woodworm, damp and contamination from previous use. Conservation is an issue that will keep recurring, whether it is because the building is in a conservation area, or in the case of redundant barns maintaining the original appearance and preserving wildlife.

It may be that the building you are intending to purchase has no planning approval to allow it to be used for residential purposes. If so, the purchase becomes dependent on obtaining permission to change the use, which in itself is a major hurdle.

The purpose of this book is primarily to assist those converting all types of redundant property to residential use and should give an insight into the various stages of the process. It is about what to look for, the numerous constraints, the cost of it all, where to get proper advice, design considerations and dealing with the local authorities. The book has been written very much with DIY in mind, but indicates how professionals can enhance and add value to the process. However, it is not intended to be a construction manual or a book on techniques, as these are available elsewhere.

For those who have little or no experience of property purchase or building, the book will assist in recognizing and dealing with every stage of the process. It will assist in understanding the various options available and which to choose. It indicates where the countless pitfalls lie and how to avoid them. It gives advice on employing professionals and builders, whilst assisting you in being able to root out 'the cowboys'. The book lets you into the world of contracts and their administration, specifications, the tender process and operations on site.

A number of Case Studies have been included to show how successful converting property can be and how the conversions were carried out. The authors wish to thank the owners for their kind cooperation and assistance. We also thank all those who contributed copyright material for the book, especially the Montresor Partnership, the Royal Institute of British Architects and the Bat Conservation Trust.

The building industry is rife with acronyms and abbreviations. Because inevitably you will be confronted with them, we have included many of them but have offered explanations or shown the origin. We have tried also to keep technical terms and jargon to a minimum but where they are included an explanation has been given.

Within Chapter 2, 'Regulations and Approvals', some reference has been made to Scotland and to the various Planning and Building Acts as they apply there. In Northern Ireland and Wales, there are also local differences. Hence, if the project is in any of these areas, you should check if there are Planning and Building Acts that have been enacted by the Local Assemblies.

Introduction to the 2010 Edition

Since the publication of the original edition in 2004 there have been numerous changes in all areas of Planning, Building Regulation and Environmental legislation, and this continues to evolve as political pressure is applied to the construction industry in response to concerns regarding climate change and sustainable development.

Technological changes in the process of applying for consents have also taken place, and it is now possible for online applications to be submitted to the new centralized Planning Portal on behalf of the relevant local authority. Planning is no longer administered by the ODPM.

Pre-application discussions and site visits with local authority officers have also been formalized, and a fee structure introduced. There are some variations in approach amongst local authorities, so all applicants are advised to make an early direct approach to navigate their way through their particular authority's current system.

Nearly all planning applications are now dealt with by the case officers up to the decision stage under delegated powers. Only exceptional or controversial projects are referred to area planning committees. Lobbying of committee members is now also discouraged, as planning policies are drafted to respond to all eventualities.

Targets in decision-making time set by central government at eight weeks have resulted in many more refusals being issued, as time is not now allowed to negotiate planning anomalies during the normal eight-week decision-making process.

Permitted development rights were also extended in October 2008 in an effort to free up planning officers' time by reducing the need for many minor extension and alteration applications. However, it is still advisable for all applicants to obtain written confirmation of permitted development rights by means of the new Lawful Development Certificate application, for which there is a reduced fee.

Environmental assessment of sites is now also obligatory so previous uses of both sites and buildings are particularly relevant in conversion projects.

Chapter 2, Regulations and Approvals, remains relevant in essence but, as can be deduced from the foregoing, changes to legislation are now being made much more frequently. However, with open government there is considerably more access for the layman by means of the internet. Therefore, if you are contemplating a conversion project our advice is to make an approach to the local authority to establish the viability of the proposal at inception.

CHAPTER 1

Basic Considerations (Getting Started)

LIFESTYLE

In considering what you want, first think about your own lifestyle and *consider* your priorities. If you do not have a property in mind already, but are thinking seriously of beginning to look for one, narrow the field by asking yourself the seemingly obvious questions: Where do you want to live? Do you prefer the country or the coast? Or would you rather be in a town or village? Why do you want to convert? With what period or style of property would you feel most comfortable? What do you intend to use the property for? As a home, a second home, a weekender, holiday house or retirement home, or are you relocating for work and therefore need it to be accessible to your place of employment? Do you like gardening, or do you want to shut the place up and forget about it until your next visit?

In looking for the right property to suit your aspirations you will no doubt have seen magazine articles or television programmes that have stirred your imagination. Translating this into reality will require some serious decisions and probably many compromises.

THE SEARCH

You will by now have decided on what you want and generally where to look; you may have studied the property pages of newspapers and magazines. Your initial search, however, should be all encompassing and thorough. Visit the local council offices and check for outline permissions granted or pending on redundant property. Purchase a large-scale map of the immediate area. Look in local papers and enquire with local estate agents. It is often the case, however, that suitable buildings will not be on the market, so you should be prepared to tour the district and look out for redundant buildings yourself, search out the owners or locals in the know and discuss possibilities with them. Buildings may have vernacular names that vary regionally, for instance 'shippen' in the north-west and 'barton' in the south-west when referring to old cattle sheds, so be prepared to learn the local names. Conversion projects are obviously as diverse as the number of building types that lend themselves with imagination to residential use.

A typical scene of derelict farmyard buildings no longer adequate for modern needs. (Nigel Rigden)

OPPOSITE: *An example of the vast space found in churches and chapels. Here a mezzanine was not permitted, which would have made the space more usable.* (Nigel Rigden)

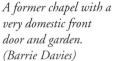

*A former chapel with a
very domestic front
door and garden.
(Barrie Davies)*

However, the majority of available buildings are at present on farms. They are often in groups where diversification or amalgamation have created redundant buildings that are too small for modern machinery and require too much maintenance for farmers to keep in good repair.

Sadly, churches and chapels are also often now redundant due to shifting population, patterns and trends in 'liturgy' and shortages of clergy. Both barns and churches offer large volumes, often with very strong and imposing structural bays which have a strict rhythm and proportion that are difficult to reduce to a domestic scale without compromising the whole.

Many barns and chapels are also listed buildings and therefore attract much more stringent planning conditions. The conversion would need to be approached in a sympathetic manner, often with much negotiation with the area's listed buildings and conservation officers and possibly the diocese. These people are there to be consulted, and the earlier this is done the less likely you are to be disappointed with the restrictions that are bound to be placed between you and the unhindered creation of your dream home.

TYPES OF PROPERTY SUITABLE FOR CONVERSION

It is possible to convert most buildings to residential use, but the most popular are agricultural buildings because of their setting and character. However, old schools and churches also provide good opportunities and architectural challenges.

The proportions of this former school were ideal for converting to residential use. (Barrie Davies)

Industrial buildings, on the other hand, are a mixed bag and can be difficult to handle, especially if the building has been contaminated by its former use. Some industrial buildings have been superbly converted; take, for example, old watermills and former railway stations. A current trend is to convert warehouse lofts for multiple occupation. Although developers mostly carry out the larger conversions, there are still opportunities for individuals. Conversions of industrial buildings can provide very desirable space close to city centres in up-and-coming formerly run-down areas. Some of the more unusual conversions are lighthouses, former banks and public houses.

LOCATION

One of the main considerations is location and aspect. If you choose a badly located property it is unlikely ever to offer a reasonable return on your investment. So, look out for busy roads, airfields, unfriendly land uses or farming practices and any other features that may cause you long-term annoyance or aggravation. If, for instance, you currently live under the Heathrow flight path and don't want to hear a plane overhead again, avoid air bases that have low-flying jets or helicopters and frequent night-time exercises. Also, you should certainly check, prior to any solicitor's search, on any planning history including proposals for future development in the locality.

Location will be important if you want nearby amenities such as a bank, post office, doctor, school, railway station, shops and so on. You might want to be within walking distance of a pub! Or you might want to be near a bus stop. You need to be able to live a sustainable lifestyle with or without transport.

This former storage building was appropriate for warehouse or loft conversion. (Nigel Rigden)

The building chosen may be surrounded by other buildings or have superb off-site views. If these views are important or there are nearby buildings, you should check at the outset whether or not you would get permission to add external openings to realize these views. If this is not possible, then this may severely restrict your ability to plan the internal accommodation as you would like and could affect your future lifestyle.

SURVEY

Having chosen your building in the right location, the next thing to do is to have it properly surveyed. If you are not familiar with building problems, then you are well advised to employ a qualified surveyor to report on the property before exchanging any contract of purchase.

This is an area, however, which causes considerable confusion due to people not being clear about what different types of survey are available or what they need. Many people take the advice of the mortgage lender or an estate agent, but it is often not clearly explained to them what the purpose of the survey is and what it will include.

The importance of choosing the appropriate survey for the type of property you're considering is crucial. A survey would be carried out normally by a building surveyor who is a corporate member of the RICS (Royal Institute of Chartered Surveyors), but you can also use architects and structural engineers (*see* Chapter 4).

Types of Survey

Valuation Survey

This is primarily to establish the market value and only provides a brief indication of any defects that would seriously affect the value of a property. Mortgage lenders require valuations to ensure that a property is good security against a mortgage. An indication is also given of the reinstatement value for insurance purposes.

This is not considered to be a structural survey and important defects could be overlooked. Most lenders will insist on this type of survey and will use their own surveyor. The cost of a valuation survey at present is in the region of £150–200.

RICS Homebuyer Survey and Valuation (HSV)

This is a basic and inexpensive service designed for properties of a conventional or normal construction. The survey is carried out to a standard format and includes an estimate of market value and a value of reinstatement for insurance purposes. It is not a detailed survey of every aspect of the property, although it should pick up any major defects. However, it may not be suitable for people converting properties.

Building Survey

This used to be known as a full structural survey and is suitable for all properties. It is a comprehensive survey especially recommended for all older buildings, all listed buildings, or a building of any period that is not of normal construction. The survey can be tailored to suit the particular circumstances. This type of survey can equally well be carried out by architects or structural engineers. What will the survey cover?

This will vary according to the scope of the work and the exact terms and conditions. Apart from a valuation survey instigated by a lender, a surveyor will normally agree the scope of the work and his fees with you in writing prior to the survey being carried out. He should also make it clear what will be included in the inspection and what will not, for example areas that are inaccessible or difficult to access without ladders and so on. He should also advise on any caveats that will apply to the inspection and subsequent report.

All types survey will include comments on the general condition and features of the property and will also indicate whether or not there is any significant defect that will affect the value, such as dry rot or subsidence. All surveys will comment on the condition of the roof structure, roof covering, gutters, chimneys, lofts, decoration, pointing and so on. A full structural survey, however, will look at the property in more detail and should include comments on insulation, drainage and services such as electricity, gas, water and heating (but only their existence and obvious condition will be noted, rather than any specific testing carried out).

If there is evidence of a problem, even a small one, a surveyor must trace it back to its origin. For example, if a damp skirting is found, the surveyor will take damp-meter readings of the floor and surrounding structures and recommend what should be done to correct the problem and whether or not

The main trusses of this derelict barn have significantly bowed and have pushed the main wall outwards. The joints in the stonework have opened up and the stones have become dislodged. Remedial action has already taken place with the insertion of metal ties. (Barrie Davies)

specialist action is required. He will also consider future maintenance of specific areas and make recommendations. He will consider the existing materials of the building and its construction and make recommendations on the suitability and compatibility of future works.

STRUCTURAL AND OTHER PROBLEMS

Among the most common faults in barns are long lengths of flanking wall unrestrained by intermediate partitions. These, coupled with poorly designed and undersized roof timbers, combine to produce outward-leaning walls and bowed timber wall plates. This can be as a result of the spread of the roof structure on to the wall plate, usually through too high a collar to restrain it. Lack of foundations and inadequate rainwater pipes and gutters may also all have contributed to this condition.

If the gable walls or end are showing signs of outward leaning, it is quite probable that the roof structure is pushing against the masonry. This condition is usually due to a lack of diagonal or wind bracing of the roof timbers and is often described as 'racking', as all members begin to lean in unison. In both of the above cases, strengthening of the roof structure to create vertical loading on to the outside walls is essential.

Constant weathering of masonry, especially on south and west walls, also has a damaging long-term affect on structures. In this situation, particularly with some soft limestone, the walls can develop outward curves, similar to drying cardboard over a very long period.

This can result in timber roof structures being pulled out of true and can require the introduction of engineered steel tension rods to stabilize the structure. Gables often need rebuilding to bring them back to the vertical and to eliminate the pulling effect.

Other roofing problems include nail sickness, whereby slates or plain tiles have begun slipping due to decayed fixings.

An example of soft limestone where the stones have been laid with their bedding planes (or strata) vertically, allowing the weather progressively to lift them off one by one. (Barrie Davies)

This can result in concentrations of water, which in turn can lead to localized wet rot and ultimately structural failure. Broken guttering can have a similar effect of concentrating water, and it is often said that no guttering is better than broken guttering. Inadequate-sized guttering also leads to frequent wetting of sections of walling and the openings below. This can in turn lead to frost damage of the damp surfaces and open up joints in the masonry or render below. 'A good hat' is essential to help maintain a dry property from above.

Moisture from the ground will happily rise 600–700mm up any external or internal wall that has been built without a damp-proof course and membrane. This rising damp in walls and floors encourages the various wood rots and mildew to develop.

Wet rot tends to develop in wooden skirtings, post ends, doorjambs and frames where constant moisture does not allow these elements to dry out. Dry rot can occur when moisture is present in unventilated pockets such as behind wooden wall panelling or in floor voids that have suffered the effects of damp. This is a problem that requires a rapid response to contain its spread, as it can ultimately destroy elements other than timber.

Tie rods, where correctly positioned and properly adjusted, will stabilize any outward movement. The picture shows an example of a tie rod, possibly contributing to the movement of the stonework. (Barrie Davies)

The timbers on this roof have decayed and bowed, allowing the tiles to be dislodged and eventually to slip downwards. (Barrie Davies)

The gutter of this barn has moved out from the edge of the roof, allowing rainwater to run directly down the face of the stonework. The water has got into the joints and along with frost has started to break down the mortar. (Barrie Davies)

Rising damp brings salts to the surface where they dry out as powders. Without treatment this makes decoration almost impossible. (Nigel Rigden)

Beetle infestation is also extremely common in older buildings, and in the case of the death-watch beetle can occur around moist ends of beams that are embedded in and supported by masonry walls. Furniture beetle is frequently found in roof and floor timbers and can ultimately lead to the weakening of the structure if left untreated. Rising damp and woodworm identification and treatment is a specialist area that can offer guarantees if remedial treatment is carried out by one of the many companies specializing in these conditions.

Lack of foundations can lead to long-term settlement of the structure, particularly on uneven sites. Poor or broken drains for rainwater dispersal can exacerbate this condition and lead to vertical cracking in the structure. If not rectifiable above ground by engineering solutions, underpinning can be considered. This is an extremely expensive but sometimes necessary solution and has to be supervised by an engineer experienced in the field. The work will also be subject to inspections by the local authority building inspector while it is in progress.

Buildings erected for animal or implement storage were not as a general rule built to the same standard of construction or with the same quality of material as their domestic and ecclesiastical contemporaries. They were also more likely to suffer infestations of vermin that could burrow into the wall crevices and voids. These are not easily discernible if concealed behind pointing or render, but can obviously cause long-term problems with water penetration, which can be very difficult to trace to source and eradicate.

PREVIOUS USE

When converting a redundant industrial or agricultural building, one of the first considerations should be to ascertain carefully what process went on or what was stored in or around it. This should also include any surrounding land, especially if you are likely to extend. Controls over contamination and pollution are very much a factor of modern life – our forefathers had little regard for the long-lasting effects of the chemicals and materials they used in manufacture or their toxic nature. Hence many buildings can hold a legacy of the past, which must be dealt with in the present.

The oak lintel on this barn door has been constantly wetted from a defective gutter above. It has then been subjected to insect attack. Note it is only the pith wood that has deteriorated, with the denser heartwood unaffected and still providing strength. (Barrie Davies)

The foundations (if any) to the corner of this barn have settled and allowed a section of stonework to break away. (Barrie Davies)

The walls of this cow barn show the marks and staining caused by generations of livestock.
(Barrie Davies)

For instance, cow barns can hold many reminders of past life in the wall structures, especially as they were often crudely rendered to a of height 1.2–1.5m for ease of washing down. The residue of salts needs to be carefully neutralized to avoid possible contamination of future decoration.

Any building or land likely to be contaminated can be identified from local planning records or even local knowledge. Watch out for names like *Tannery Lane* and *Station Road*, as these will give clues to previous uses.

Likely contaminated buildings and sites would include:

- railway buildings, especially workshops
- tanneries
- agricultural buildings used for storing fertilizers and pesticides or for housing animals

The decoration on this wall has broken down and is being pushed off by the various salts and contamination present in the stonework.
(Barrie Davies)

- paper and printing works
- military buildings
- industrial buildings where chemicals were used stored or produced
- graveyards
- buildings constructed from asbestos materials.

Signs of possible contamination would include:

- lack of vegetation, stunted or unnatural growth
- surface materials with unusual colours or oily and tarry stains
- patches of diesel or other oil spillage
- fumes and odours of an unnatural nature indicating the presence of organic compounds and corrosive substances
- natural odours indicating the waste products from animals
- drums, containers or tanks, whether full or not, which may have contained various chemicals or oils. The labels, if present, should give some clue as to what was contained within them.

If any of these indicators show contaminants may be present, then there is a duty to advise the local Environmental Health Officer (EHO). He or she will arrange for tests to be carried out in order to establish whether or not contaminants are present, and, if so, what types and in what quantities. He or she will also advise how they should be treated, for example by removal, filling or sealing. You will also be advised that any contaminated materials or soil removed from the site are required to be disposed of at a licensed tipping site, otherwise you are liable to face a heavy fine.

Some contaminants, however, give no obvious indication, particularly radon and methane gas, which have no colour or odour. Radon is a naturally occurring, radioactive gas that is produced when uranium or radium decays. The most common occurrence is in parts of the West Country, Northamptonshire and Derbyshire. The gas over a long time can increase the risk of lung cancer unless special precautions are taken in the construction of buildings. Guidance on testing for radon and adapting buildings to alleviate its affects and the exact geographical areas affected can be obtained from the

This street sign is self-evident. Also look out for others such as Gas Lane, Tanyard and Quarry Lane. (Barrie Davies)

National Radiological Protection Board (*see* References) or the local building inspector.

Methane is commonly found associated with landfill sites. It is a gas that will burn or explode and can also asphyxiate. Special measures need to be adopted in any construction near landfill sites and initial advice can be sought from the local building inspector.

A contaminant, which has been causing increasing public concern, is asbestos. There has been a considerable rise in the number of deaths caused by it, with the numbers projected to rise even further in the coming years. Asbestos is a naturally occurring fibre, which has three distinct forms: blue (Crocidolite), brown (Amosite) and white (Chrysotile). The most toxic are the blue and brown forms, though recently white has come to be considered equally dangerous. Asbestos is inherently non-flammable and has excellent heat-insulating properties and prior to the ban on the importation and use of blue and brown asbestos in 1985 and white in 1999, it was commonly used in sheet form for fireproof linings and floor tiles. It was also used in the lagging of hot-water pipework and boilers and fire protection to structural steelwork. The white form of asbestos has always been associated with corrugated asbestos-cement roof panels and until comparatively recently these were still being produced.

A barn with a sheet roof constructed from asbestos-cement. (Barrie Davies)

When asbestos is suspected in a building the EHO will insist on tests being taken to determine which type of asbestos is present and to ascertain how much contamination is present in the surrounding air. If the contamination exceeds the amount permitted under the regulations or the asbestos is damaged or is integral with the proposed works then it has to be removed. This will need to be carried out by a properly licensed contractor and disposed of only at a licensed tip. Asbestos that is sound, however, can remain provided that no work is carried out to it and it is clearly marked with a proprietary label as a future warning to anyone that may work on the building.

Another issue in rural areas can be foot-and-mouth disease. Its eradication has left some parts of the country blighted and farms unsaleable. Here there is no solution and any buildings that have been associated with the disease are best avoided for the foreseeable future.

COMMON MISTAKES

If you are new to building, or even if you have some experience, then you are as likely as not to run into some of the problems associated with any building project. Some of the most common are:

Doing It Yourself

If you are intending to do the building work yourself it is quite common to overestimate the amount of work that you can reasonably do and the time it takes. You may think that you have the necessary skills to do most things, but in practice this may not be the case. This is a fact borne out by the number of television programmes showing the difficulties people with limited building abilities have got themselves into. Often DIY is a false economy if you are unskilled, inefficient and disorganized.

Managing the Project

Spending too much time on a project can jeopardize family life and create problems with your daytime job. Whilst small DIY elements carried out in one's spare time may cause little problem, managing the project on a daily basis will necessitate meetings with subcontractors and many visits to check progress and solve problems. This is especially difficult from a distance unless you employ the services of project supervisor, for example an architect. Another problem of managing a project yourself can be poor quality control, especially if you lack experience in building.

Budget

Not setting a realistic budget at the start is one of the most common problems and can lead to you running out of cash and needing to seek additional finance. It is a mistake to use average building prices. If the budget is exceeded it can lead to false economies, or having to do the work yourself, or the need to downgrade specifications.

Changing Plans

Changing plans during the later design stage or in the construction phases invariably leads to increased costs. You can be caught out by 'add backs', even when you think you are omitting an item. The contractor may have already prepared the site for something, or have ordered and paid for an item that you later omit. Changing the plans without consulting the planners is also an area that can lead to difficulty, even if you regard the change as being of a minor nature.

Planning and Building Regulations

Not understanding the basics of planning and the

The interior of a barn in its original condition. (Montresor Partnership)

The only thing in this picture that is vertical is the telegraph post. This is probably helping to keep the wall from moving any further. (Barrie Davies)

Building Regulations often leads to disappointment and sometimes conflict if your ideas are unrealistic. Starting work before receipt of the necessary approvals is also a common mistake.

No Formal Contract

Having no formal contract with a builder or subcontractor usually leads to issues at the final account stage, especially if no firm price was agreed at the outset.

Payments

Not understanding how to evaluate the correct payments to contractors and subcontractors and paying too much in advance. It is almost impossible to get work put right if you have actually paid for it.

Paying in advance can leave you high and dry if the contractor fails to perform or does not turn up. Another problem can be assessing timing of payments with consequent cash flow difficulties and the chances of running out of cash.

ASSESSING THE BUILDING AND SITE

A simple checklist should include some or all of the things to watch out for when visiting any site and when making further investigations.

Initial Condition

If the building is derelict or vacant you may be put off initially by its condition and by the litter and debris found lying around.

This is the moment for vision, not panic. Try to imagine the structure fully restored, with new floors, new windows and perhaps a fully landscaped garden. Then imagine yourself living there and work out what spaces should go where and what views you should get. If this works, then you are over the first hurdle!

Structure and Ground Conditions

A quick walk around any property checking for straightness and verticality of walls will soon reveal if there are active problems with the structure.

You should also check the roof for bowing or rotting timbers.

Have a look at any adjoining properties as well for signs of structural movement. A check should be made with the local authority to see if there are any records of mining or quarrying in the area or of any adverse ground conditions that might affect future extensions. This will ascertain whether the problems are common and due to ground conditions. Also check whether any trees present are causing or are likely to cause ground movement, which can affect building foundations and drains.

If at first sight there appear to be structural problems it is probably the right time to call in a surveyor or engineer for at least an initial appraisal and advice on whether the problems are insurmountable or solutions can be found.

This barn roof shows the effect of sagging rafters, purlins and ridge board. The trusses, represented by the high points, are supporting the roof on the original line. (Barrie Davies)

Planning

Check with the local Planning Authority as to the planning status of the building and site. Are there any existing permissions? Is it in a conservation area or is it listed? Can the use be changed to residential? Also check whether there are proposals or permissions on surrounding land or properties, for example new roads, housing estates, industrial development and so on. Watch for anything that might be detrimental to the future value and spoil your enjoyment of the converted property.

Previous Use

Apart from agricultural buildings, the sites of the manufacture and storage of toxic chemicals and heavy metals are mostly known about and documented by local authorities and the Environment Agency, and should show up on the initial searches for the conveyance. Decontamination is a very specialized and hence costly operation; properties with a possible history of unfriendly uses should therefore probably be avoided.

You should check what the building and site have been used for as far back as you can go. You should also check for buildings that may have been demolished on the site, as these could have been contaminated and traces could still be present in the soil.

Boundaries

It is quite common to misunderstand what the boundaries are and who owns them. A good solicitor will be able to help, although as often as not the deeds of a property can be silent on the subject. You should check key dimensions to any fixed boundaries and whether or not the boundary of any hedge or wall is the centre line or to one side. This will avoid future problems. Check for adverse possession such as fences being moved to encroach on the land or unauthorized occupation.

Access

Has the building and site got a suitable and adequately sized vehicular access, and if so is it adopted? Does the access comply with the highway regulations – for instance, if it joins a main road, are there adequate sight lines at the junction? If not, do you need additional land to achieve these? Are there any rights of way over the access?

Pollution

Check whether there is any likely source of pollution nearby. This would include smells and noise from adjacent farms and dairies. Check out noise from any busy roads, railways, aircraft, factories, workshops and neighbours' hi-fi systems. It is also a good idea to visit the site at different times to ascertain if and when potential nuisances occur.

Drainage

Is mains drainage connected? If not, will it be possible to connect the foul and surface water to

The water in the river around this mill looks perfectly calm and innocuous. However, the mill floods every year and the owner marks the wall in the basement to show the levels reached and keeps any vital equipment above these levels. (Nigel Rigden)

mains drainage? Do levels and gradients allow for it to discharge by gravity alone? Will you need to install a septic tank or cesspit? Is there sufficient room on site for treated effluent to drain away? Does the drainage need to cross over a neighbour's property or join into their system? If so, will you be faced with needing to pay financial compensation?

Mains Services

Are the mains services connected? If not, you should check the cost and feasibility of providing mains services, especially if the nearest connection points are some way away and perhaps over adjoining land. Early enquiries to the service providers are highly recommended in order to obtain a clear indication of the likely cost of providing a mains supply and indeed if it is possible.

Flooding

Does the site have a history of flooding? Is the site on a flood plain and is there a watercourse or river nearby? The Environment Agency will be able to assist in pin-pointing likely trouble spots. Visit the site if you can when it is raining to see if there could be any build-up of surface water, and to check that the drains function properly and any watercourse can cope.

Footpaths

It is essential to check if there are any footpaths crossing the site. Ordnance Survey maps are useful in the first instance and show most public footpaths in existence. If there is one, consider what affect it is going to have on your privacy and daily life. Realigning or moving a public footpath takes considerable time and is a complicated process, with no guarantee of success. So if the presence of a footpath is likely to annoy you, consider an alternative location.

Trees

If there are any trees on the site that you intend to remove, then check there are no Tree Preservation Orders (TPOs) in force. This is especially important in conservation areas. If you prune or fell without consent a tree that is protected by a TPO or is in a conservation area, you may be liable to a hefty fine.

An active bat roost. (John Kaczanow & The Bat Conservation Trust)

Wildlife

Redundant farm buildings can be refuges for many different species of protected wildlife such as bats, owls, badgers and so on. These have to be treated in accordance with the regulations enforced by the Statutory Nature Conservation Organizations (SNCOs), for example English Nature. Take a good look around for active nests and burrows (*see* Chapter 2).

Value

You should be mindful of what the value of the converted property is likely to be when completed, especially if you ever need to sell. There is always a ceiling on value, which is normally affected by location and the demand within an area. It is therefore important at the outset to discuss potential values with a local estate agent. This will help to ensure that the sum of the purchase price of the property and the cost of the conversion works is targeted some way below future market value.

Useful Information and Contacts

- Environment Agency – *www.environment-agency.gov.uk/ subjects/flood*
- English Nature Tel. 01733 455000 – *www.english-nature.org.uk*
- National Radiological Protection Board Tel. 0800 614529 – *www.nrpb.org/radon*

CHAPTER 2

Regulations and Approvals

Before you commence any works there are a number of Acts and Regulations to be considered. Under these, you are very likely to be required to make applications to various statutory bodies for permission prior to carrying out any building alterations, demolitions and so on. Whilst it is very worthwhile having a brief understanding about what they contain and what they mean, it is strongly recommended that you seek professional advice on all but the simplest projects. Those that are most likely to affect conversion works are:

- The Town and Country Planning Act 1947
- The Planning (Listed Buildings and Conservation Areas) Act
- The Building Regulations.

Other regulations, which you may come across and will need to be considered, are:

- The Party Wall Act
- Construction (Design and Management) Regulations.

PLANNING PERMISSION

The Town and Country Planning Act 1947 brought the modern planning system into being. It ensured that the development of land and buildings was controlled in the public interest and enforced consistently across the UK. It created local planning authorities and required the preparation of development plans indicating the manner in which land in their area should be used. All land was made subject to planning control and the Planning Authority was given powers to deal with development carried out without planning permission. The authorities were also given powers to secure the preservation of trees and buildings of architectural or historic interest and to control the display of advertisements. Subsequent legislation has progressively strengthened the provisions for enforcing planning control and the provisions relating to the preservation of buildings of special architectural or historic interest. Also the Environment Act 1995 provided for the Environment Agency, which became responsible for the control of pollution and waste, the National Rivers Auhority and the setting up of the National Parks as distinct planning authorities.

Planning permission is normally required to carry out the following:

- Carrying out building operations. These include new buildings and external alterations or extensions to existing buildings. These also include demolitions and rebuilding.
- Material change of use.
- Building something that is at variance with the original planning permission, or to retain something that was built without permission.
- Splitting up a property to provide more than one home or dividing it up to use part as a business premises.
- Any work that might obstruct the view of road users. Any changes to an existing vehicular access to a highway or formation of a new one.
- Departures from the Local Development Plan.

Planning Permissions

There are several types of planning permission. The ones specifically relating to the Town and Country Planning Act 1990 (in Scotland the 1997 Act) are:

- **Outline Planning Consent** This is a preliminary consent, which gives approval to the general arrangements and basic form of any proposed development. This is likened to 'dipping one's toe in the water'. This does not normally permit you to proceed with any of the work on site until the 'Approval of Reserved Matters' (matters reserved for future consideration). You have three years from the date of the granting of outline permission to make an application for 'Approval of Reserved Matters'.
- **Approval of Reserved Matters** Following outline consent, detailed plans and elevations of the works proposed, including proposed materials, are submitted to obtain a full planning consent. Reserved matters usually include siting, design, external appearance, means of access and the landscaping of the site.
- **Full Planning Consent** This is where a detailed application is made at the outset without going through the outline and reserved matters stage. This is the normal route taken, especially if your proposals are not too controversial and you have been given positive indications by the planning department. The duration of a full permission is five years from the date on which it was granted.
- **Change of Use Consent** This is another form of full planning consent, where the existing or previous use does not relate to the use proposed in the application. This route will normally be taken by people converting property. Again Full Plans and elevations of the

proposal need to be submitted. *There is no outline stage available when changes of use are proposed.*

The types of planning permission that relate to the Planning (Listed Buildings and Conservation Areas) Act 1990 (in Scotland the 1997 Act) are:

- **Listed Building Consent** Where this applies, it is required in addition to any other permission.
- **Conservation Area Consent** As with Listed Building Consent, this is an additional permission.

There are also Permitted Development Rights under the Town and Country Planning General Permitted Development Order 1995. This allows you to carry out certain building works without the need for permission and the following are a few examples:

- Extensions up to 115m³ are allowed provided they are no nearer a highway than the original building or at least 20m away, whichever is the closest. If the extension is within 2m of the boundary, it must not exceed 4m in height or the height of the original building.
- Installation of dormer windows not exceeding 50m³ in total.
- Roof lights, doors and windows: these are only allowed if done in isolation and not as part of a planning application. The advice is to get your permission first without a window or door and put them in later, provided there is no restriction on the approval.
- Sheds, outbuildings, swimming pools, hard standings and home office: these are considered ancillary to the home.
- Porches.

APPLYING FOR PLANNING PERMISSION

Applying for planning permission is relatively straightforward. Initially, you should contact the local planning office and talk over what you intend to do and obtain their advice. Nowadays some planning offices are not well staffed and it is increasingly difficult to obtain advice and meet with a planning

officer, but you will certainly be able to obtain the appropriate application forms and be advised on the application fee required. Typical current planning application forms are shown on pages 30–33.

You should also consult the Local Development Plan for the area to see what criteria or restrictions have been placed on development, for example Green Belt, or what uses have been designated and what is

South Somerset District Council
APPLICATION FOR
PLANNING PERMISSION

For Office Use Only

PLEASE ANSWER QUESTIONS
IN BLOCK CAPITAL

Application No.	
Fee Received	
Date Registered	

---

1. Name and address of applicant

Tel. No. _____

2. Name and address of agent

Tel. No. _____
Personal contact name_____

---

3. Address of property to which application relates (if different from applicant address) shown edged red on the site plan and block plan

Site area (hectares) _____

4. What is the applicant's interest in the land? (e.g. owner, lessee, prospective purchaser, etc.)

---

5. Does the applicant own or control any adjoining land? If so, indicate the area edged blue on the site plan and block plan

6. Brief description of proposal

---

7. If the proposal is for residential development, state the number and type of dwelling units proposed

8. Indicate whether the proposal involves the following:

☐ New building(s)
☐ Alteration or extension
☐ Change of use
☐ Construction of a new access to a highway (vehicular)
☐ Construction of a new access to a highway (pedestrian)
☐ Alteration of an existing access to a highway (vehicular)

9a Indicate whether the application is for:

☐ Outline planning permission

☐ Approval of reserved matters

☐ Full planning permission

☐ Renewal of temporary permission

☐ Removal of condition(s)

9b If outline permission, delete any of the following which are not reserved for subsequent approval:

Siting/Design/External appearance/Means of access/ Landscaping

If full planning permission, say if you are applying to retain existing buildings or continue existing uses
_____

If approval of reserved matters, state the date and number of outline permission and which reserved matters
_____

If renewal of temporary permission or removal of condition, state the date and number of previous permission or identify the particular condition
_____

10. State the present use of buildings/land. If vacant, state last previous use and date when last so used.

_____
_____
_____

11. Does the proposal involve the felling of any trees?

Yes   No

If yes, specify type and number

_____

12. Drainage

(a) How will surface water be disposed of?

_____
_____
_____
_____
_____

(b) Foul sewage will be disposed of to:-

Existing   Main sewer   Septic tank

New   Cesspit   Other

Not applicable

13. State type and colour of all external materials of walls and roof

_____
_____
_____

14. Building Regulations. A separate application for building regulations consent has already been made.

Yes [   ]   No [   ]

If no, please check with the Building Control Unit to establish if an application is required.

If the application is for industrial, office, warehousing, storage, shopping or other commercial purposes, please complete questions 15 to 21 below. If not, continue with question 22.

15. In the case of industrial development, give a description of the processes to be carried on, and of the end products, and the type of plant or machinery to be installed.

_____
_____
_____

16.
(a) If the proposal forms a stage of a larger scheme for which planning permission is not at present sought, please give what information you can about the ultimate development.
(b) Is the proposal related to an existing use on or near the site? If yes, please explain the relationship.
(c) Is this a proposal to replace existing premises in this area or elsewhere which have become obsolete, inadequate or otherwise unsatisfactory? If yes, please give details including gross floor area of such premises and state your intentions in respect of those premises.

_____
_____
_____
_____
_____
_____
_____
_____
_____

17. Please give details of floor space

	Existing floor space m²	Lost floor space m²	Additional floor space m²
(a) What is the total floor space of all buildings to which the application relates?			
(b) What is the amount of industrial floor space included in the above figure?	____	____	____
(c) What is the amount of office floor space?	____	____	____
(d) What is the amount of floor space for retail trading?	____	____	____
(e) What is the amount of floor space for storage?	____	____	____
(f) What is the amount of floor space for warehousing?	____	____	____
(g) What is the amount of floor space for other commercial development?	____	____	____

31

18. Please give details of staff numbers   Existing staff   Additional staff

(a) Office

(b) Industrial

(c) Other

19. What is the estimated vehicular traffic flow to the site during a normal working day? (Please include all vehicles except those used by individual employees driving to work).

20. What is the nature, volume and proposed means of disposal of any trade effluents or trade refuse?

21. Will the proposal involve the use of storage of any of the materials of type and quantity referred to in Note H. If yes, state materials and approximate quantities.

22. Does the proposal involve the importation on site of any waste or bulk fill materials such as clay and soils?

Yes   No

If yes, please indicate the type and quantity

23. What waste material will be generated on site during construction and where will this go or how will it be used?

Please indicate type and quantity of waste material

24. List the drawings and plans submitted with this application. (See Guidance Notes)

25. I/We hereby apply for

Planning permission to carry out the development described in this application and the accompanying plans.

Planning permission to retain buildings or works already constructed or carried out, or a use of land already taking place as described in this application and the accompanying plans.

Approval of details of the matters that were reserved in the outline permission which is referred to in 9 above.

Check list. Please ensure you submit:

Five copies of the completed application forms

Five copies of all plans (See Note C in Guidance Notes)

One completed ownership certificate (Article 7) (see over)

Enclose the appropriate fee of £_____ (made payable to South Somerset District Council)

Sign and date the form below

Signed _____ on behalf of _____ Date _____

Additional Information

Certificates and Notices under Article 7 of the Town and Country Planning (General Development Procedure) Order 1995. The appropriate certificate must accompany the application unless you are seeking approval for reserved matters. Before completing, please read Note D in the Notes for Applicants. Only one copy need be completed. (In the certificates, the term "owner" means a person having a freehold interest or a leasehold interest, the unexpired term of which was not less than seven years).

Certificate A

I/We hereby certify that:

1.   No person other than the applicant(s) was an owner of any part of the land to which the application relates at the beginning of the period of 21 days ending with the date of the accompanying application.

Delete one or other of the alternatives to paragraph 2, not both, otherwise the certificate will not be valid.

*2.   None of the land to which the application relates constitutes or forms part of agricultural holding under separate tenancy.

*2.   The requisite notice has been served on the following, who for the period of 21 days ending with the date of the application, was a tenant of any agricultural holding any part of which was comprised in the land to which the application relates, viz:-

Name of Tenant   Address   _____   Date of Service of Notice(s)

_____   _____   _____

3.   No person other than the applicant is entitled to an interest in a relevant mineral in the land.

Signed _____   **Date** _____

*On behalf of _____

Certificate B

I/We hereby certify that:

1.   The requisite notice has been served on all other persons who for the period of 21 days ending with the date of the accompanying application were owners of any land to which the application relates, viz:-

Name of Owner   Address   _____   Date of Service of Notice(s)

_____   _____   _____

*2.   None of the land to which the application relates constitutes or forms part of agricultural holding under separate tenancy.

*2.   The requisite notice has been served on the following, who for the period of 21 days ending with the date of the application, was a tenant of any agricultural holding any part of which was comprised in the land to which the application relates, viz:-

Name of Tenant   Address   _____   Date of Service of Notice(s)

_____   _____   _____

3.   The requisite notice has been served on all other persons who for the period of 21 days ending with the date of the application were persons entitled to an interest in a relevant mineral in the land to which the application relates, viz:-

Name of person with mineral   Address   _____   Date of Service of Notice(s)
Interest

_____   _____   _____

Signed _____   **Date** _____

*On behalf of _____

The forms on pages 30–33 are typical of current planning application forms. The local authorities publish guides to help complete them. The certificates must be filled in correctly, otherwise the application will be rejected. (South Somerset District Council)

Planning Flow Chart

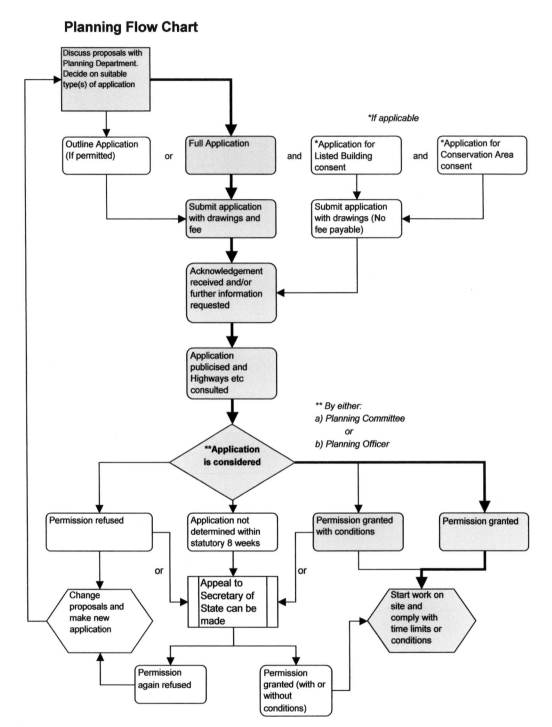

The diagram shows the path a typical application will take. It also indicates alternatives and loops in the process. (Barrie Davies)

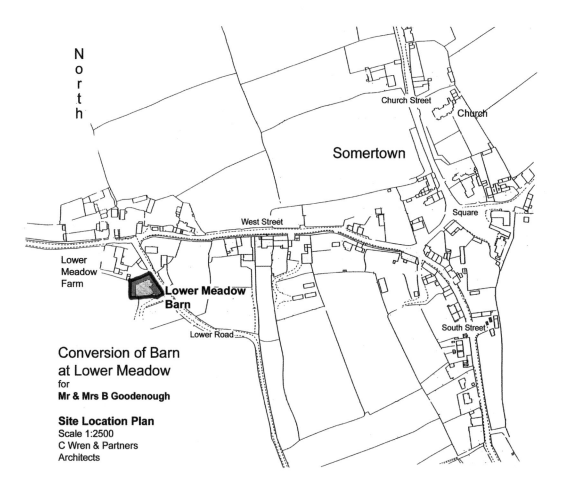

North

Church Street

Church

Somertown

West Street

Square

Lower
Meadow
Farm

Lower Meadow Barn

Lower Road

South Street

**Conversion of Barn
at Lower Meadow**
for
Mr & Mrs B Goodenough

Site Location Plan
Scale 1:2500
C Wren & Partners
Architects

The site location plan, as its name suggests, indicates the location of the site in its locality. It should show it in the context of any nearby town or village for ease of reference. (Barrie Davies)

likely to be permitted. You will soon know whether or not your proposals are contentious and at variance with local policy. It is worth checking that there are development rights available to allow you to extend. You should also check whether or not the building is listed or in a conservation area. (It is now possible with most local authorities to be able to download the relevant application forms and development plans direct from the Internet.)

You will need to decide what form of application is appropriate to your circumstances. If you are sure the proposals have a good chance of being approved, then a full application is the preferred option.

If you are less certain, then an outline application is the better alternative, though this may not always be accepted for conversion works. However, you will only need to submit a location plan, site plan and some basic sketch drawings with an outline application. It is always a good idea to choose an architect with a record in dealing with the local planning department, especially one that has been recommended by them and has been able to obtain permissions with the minimum of fuss.

The full application will need to be accompanied by drawings, which will at least need to include a location plan showing the site and its surroundings at

35

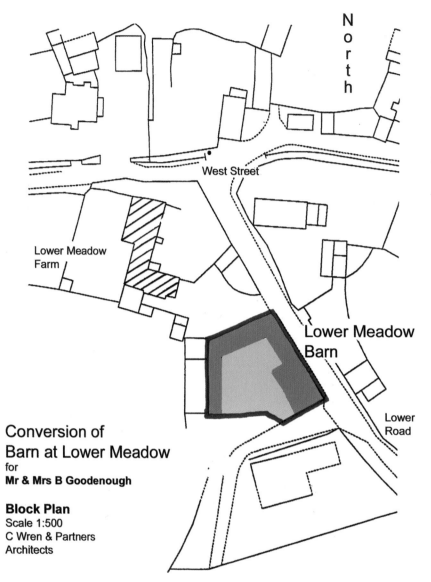

Lower Meadow
Farm

West Street

North

Lower Meadow
Barn

Lower
Road

The block plan shows the site and the buildings on it. It will show any neighbouring properties and local roads. The site is normally edged red and any adjoining property owned by the applicant, not forming part of the application, is edged blue. (Barrie Davies)

Conversion of Barn at Lower Meadow
for
Mr & Mrs B Goodenough

Block Plan
Scale 1:500
C Wren & Partners
Architects

a scale of 1:2,500 or 1:1,250 and a block plan of the site at a scale of 1:500.

Other drawings that would be required are plans and elevations of the existing building along with the proposed plans and elevations. Sometimes, in addition a sectional drawing would be required to show the proposals more clearly along with sample materials. All these detailed drawings should be at least drawn to 1:100 scale and sometimes 1:50 depending on the local authority.

Presentation is very important and your proposals should be clear and the drawings as precise and as attractive as possible. It is no use thinking that drawings produced with amateur computer packages will be as good as professionally produced ones. Good drawings will assist the planner, who, after all, is very busy, and the members of the planning committee to appreciate fully your proposals.

Once the application has been submitted it is normally acknowledged in one of two ways. Firstly,

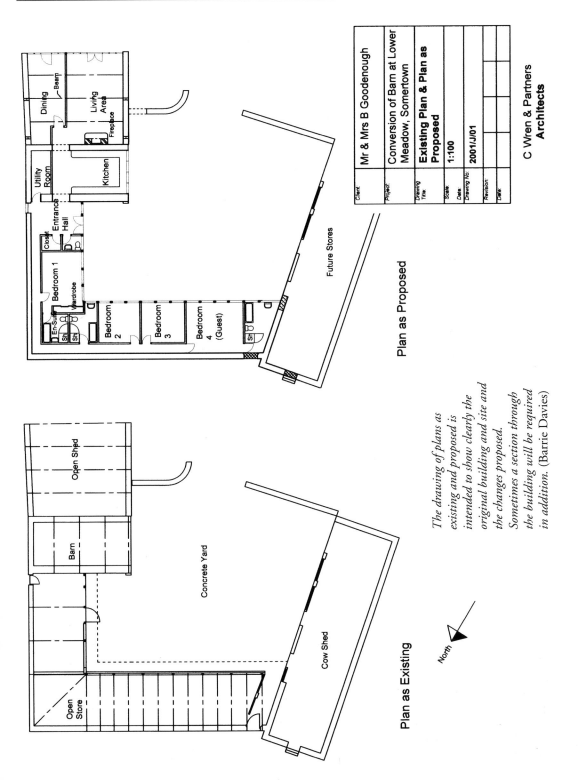

Client:	Mr & Mrs B Goodenough
Project:	Conversion of Barn at Lower Meadow, Somertown
Drawing Title:	**Existing Plan & Plan as Proposed**
Scale:	1:100
Date:	
Drawing No:	2001/J/01
Revision:	
Date:	

C Wren & Partners
Architects

Plan as Proposed

Dining
Beam
Living Area
Fireplace
Utility Room
Kitchen
Entrance Hall
Closet
Bedroom 1
Wardrobe
En-Suite
Sh Sh
Bedroom 2
Bedroom 3
Bedroom 4 (Guest)
Sh
Future Stores

The drawing of plans as existing and proposed is intended to show clearly the original building and site and the changes proposed. Sometimes a section through the building will be required in addition. (Barrie Davies)

Plan as Existing

Open Shed
Barn
Open Store
Concrete Yard
Cow Shed

North

37

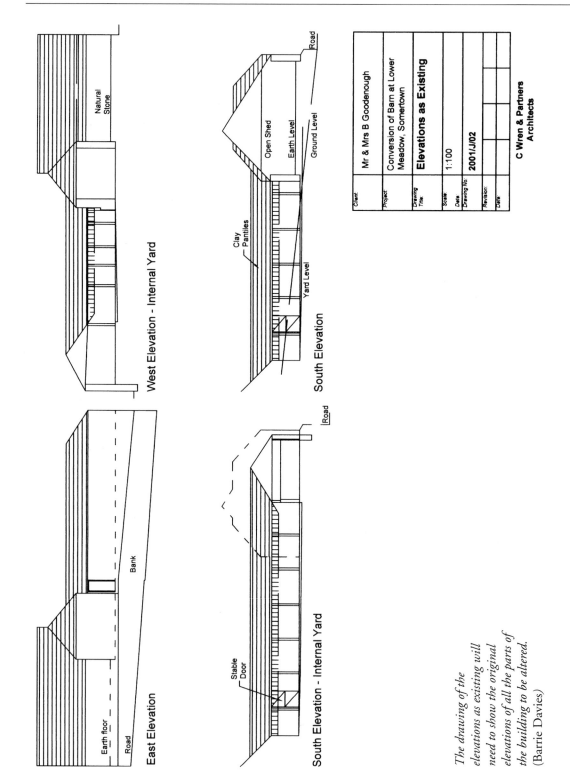

West Elevation - Internal Yard

Natural Stone

East Elevation

Earth floor
Road
Bank

South Elevation

Road
Clay Pantiles
Open Shed
Earth Level
Ground Level
Yard Level

South Elevation - Internal Yard

Road
Stable Door

Client:	Mr & Mrs B Goodenough			
Project:	Conversion of Barn at Lower Meadow, Somertown			
Drawing Title:	**Elevations as Existing**			
Scale:	1:100			
Date:				
Drawing No:	2001/J/02			
Revision:				
Date:				

C Wren & Partners
Architects

The drawing of the elevations as existing will need to show the original elevations of all the parts of the building to be altered. (Barrie Davies)

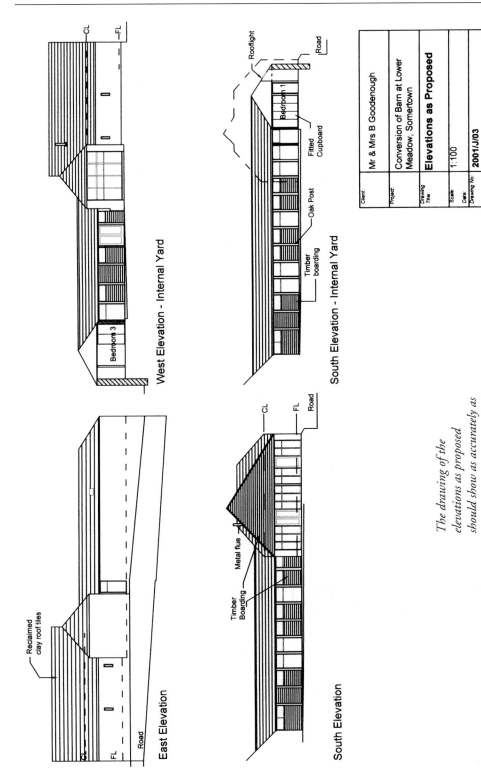

West Elevation - Internal Yard

South Elevation - Internal Yard

East Elevation

South Elevation

The drawing of the elevations as proposed should show as accurately as possible the changes proposed to elevations and indicate the materials to be used and their colour. (Barrie Davies)

Client:	Mr & Mrs B Goodenough
Project:	Conversion of Barn at Lower Meadow, Somertown
Drawing Title:	**Elevations as Proposed**
Scale:	1:100
Date:	
Drawing No:	**2001/J/03**
Revision:	
Date:	

C Wren & Partners Architects

you may be asked to provide further information and told that the application is invalid until it is provided, or secondly, if all is in order, you would be advised that it has been placed on the Planning Register. You will receive a letter of receipt for the application and will be advised of the date that a decision is to be reached. Once it is on the register there is a requirement for the local authority to determine your application within eight weeks unless your written permission is obtained to extend this period.

Once your application is on the register any interested party can inspect it at the local council offices. The local authority will also inform your neighbours and will put up a notice on or near the site. The local authority will also seek to consult other bodies such as the Highways Department, Environment Agency and Parish Council.

The planning department will usually prepare a report for larger proposals with recommendations for the planning committee to consider. This committee is made up of a number of local councillors. Frequently, the committee gives delegated powers to the planning department to determine applications on its behalf, especially for works of minor alteration or extension where there is no objection. It is extremely important to keep in touch with the officer dealing with your application in order that an indication can be gained on whether or not there is any likelihood of the scheme being refused. If you are aware of issues prior to the committee stage then you can make suitable modifications, up to three days before the meeting, to enable the application to be reconsidered. You can also lobby your local councillors or MP for support if you think there are likely to be problems. You can also ask for a deferral and suggest a meeting on site at which you can put your side in context. But be prepared to negotiate and accept compromise or accept conditions that are not too onerous. You may need to suspend or withdraw an application to reconsider your position. It is certainly better to do this than receive an outright refusal at the first attempt! You need to be proactive, but do not lose your temper and feel that the planners have taken against you personally. Planning regulations are not always black and white and planning officers can interpret them and the council's policy in different ways, so try to work with them

and ask their advice, even if you feel totally frustrated by the system.

Should the local authority not determine your application within the statutory time limit or you receive a refusal of planning permission, then you have the right to appeal to the Secretary of State. This is a final resort and appeals usually take several months to decide. The local authority must give reasons for its refusal or for imposing conditions.

LISTED BUILDINGS CONSENT

Listed buildings are categorized as those that have special architectural or historic interest.

You will require Listed Building Consent if the any of the following situations apply:

- you intend to demolish a listed building
- you intend to alter or extend a listed building in such a manner that would affect its character as a building of special architectural or historic interest.

You will also be expected to have Listed Building Consent for any works that separate buildings in the grounds of a listed building. It is a criminal offence to carry out any work to a listed building without prior

This bell on a former school had to be recast and the belfry restored. (Barrie Davies)

consent and carries a penalty of up to two years' imprisonment. A local authority can issue an enforcement notice to stop the work and demand that you restore the building to its former state.

What Can be Listed?

Listing can include any structure and any part of a building, but does not necessarily include plant or machinery contained in a building. The building's exterior is by far the most common reason for listing, if it contributes to the architectural or historic interest of any group of buildings of which it forms a part. Also any feature of the building can be listed if it consists of a man-made object or structure fixed to it, such as an altar, or it forms part of the land and is comprised within the curtilage, for example tombs.

Procedure for Obtaining Listed Buildings Consent

This is very similar to applying for planning permission, except that there is no outline stage and no fee is payable. The application is made on a form obtainable from the local authority and is accompanied by sufficient information to identify the building and such drawings necessary to describe the proposed works.

Should the local authority intend granting permission to Grade I and II* buildings, then the Secretary of State must be notified, also if permission is to be granted to demolish a Grade II structure. This allows him to call in the application for his own decision. As with planning, there is a right of appeal against refusal. It is likely for any Listed Building Consent given that conditions will be made regarding the preservation of original features, the making good of any damage to the building caused by the works and the reconstruction of the building or any part with the use of original materials as far as is practical.

CONSERVATION AREA CONSENT

The local authority has a duty under the Planning Act to determine areas of special architectural or historic interest in order to preserve and enhance the essential character or appearance. Designation of

---

Listed Buildings

Listed buildings (or protected buildings) are scheduled in one of the following categories:

- **Grade I** – these are buildings of exceptional interest (approximately 2 per cent of all listed buildings are in this category)
- **Grade II*** – these are particularly important buildings of more than special interest, but not in the exceptional category (about 4 per cent of listed buildings)
- **Grade II** – these are buildings of special interest, but not sufficiently important to be counted among the best.

(In Northern Ireland, there is no statutory grading, but the Environment and Heritage Service operates an internal grading system.)

The criteria for listing cover the following groups:

- all buildings built before 1700 which survive in anything like their original condition are listed
- most buildings built between 1700 and 1840 are listed, though selection is required
- between 1840 and 1914 only those buildings of defined quality and character are listed
- between 1914 and a date thirty years prior to the present day selected buildings of high quality are listed.

(From the above you will realize that most ecclesiastical buildings are likely to be listed.)

It should be noted that economic factors are not taken into account when considering whether or not to list a building. However, the cost of repairs and maintenance, and whether the building can be converted to an economic use, are matters that can be considered by the local authority when dealing with applications for Listed Buildings Consent.

South Somerset District Council

APPLICATION FOR LISTED BUILDING CONSENT/ CONSERVATION AREA CONSENT

For Office Use Only	
Application No.	
Date Registered	

PLEASE ANSWER QUESTIONS IN BLOCK CAPITALS

1. Name and Address of applicant Tel no.	2. Name and address of agent Tel No. (Personal Contact Name)
3. Address of property to which application relates if different from applicant address.	4. Applicants Interest e.g. owner, lessee etc.
5. Description of the proposed works	6. State Type, colour and finishes of all external materials to be used a) Walls b) Roof covering c) Windows and Doors
7. Has Grant Aid been applied for? Yes ☐ No ☐ If yes please give details	8. List of plans/photographs submitted
9. Has a separate application for planning permission been made? Yes ☐ No ☐	10. Has a separate application for building regulations approval been made? Yes ☐ No ☐

11. Check list. Please ensure you submit:

Three copies of the completed application forms
Three copies of all plans/photographs
One completed ownership certificate (Regulation 6, see over)
Sign and date the form below

Signed _____ **on behalf of** _____ **Date** _____

The Listed Building and Conservation Area consent application forms are combined.
They must be completed in addition to the normal planning form and certificates.
(South Somerset District Council)

PLANNING (LISTED BUILDINGS AND CONSERVATION AREAS) ACT 1990

**PLANNING (LISTED BUILDINGS AND CONSERVATION AREAS)
REGULATIONS 1990 (No. 1519)**

Certificates under Regulation 6

Certificate A

I hereby certify that no person other than the applicant was the owner of any part of the land to which the application relates at the beginning of the period of 21 days ending with the date of the application.

Signed _____ **on behalf of** _____ **date** _____

Certificate B

I hereby certify that the requisite notice has been given to all those persons, other than the applicant, who at the beginning of the period of 21 days ending with the date of the application were owners of the land to which the application relates.

Name of owner _____

Address _____

_____

_____

_____

Date of Service of Notice _____

Signed _____ **on behalf of** _____ **date** _____

A window on this former school had to be carefully restored by stonemasons using stone taken from a local quarry. (Barrie Davies)

such an area gives the local authority considerable additional powers over the use and development of land in the area. It is always worthwhile talking to the local conservation officer prior to making any application. It is normally the requirement of the local authority that only full planning applications are considered in conservation areas because design is such a crucial matter that it cannot be considered under reserved matters. If you intend conversion of a building within such an area you will need Conservation Area Consent to carryout the following:

• demolish a building with a volume of more than 115m^3
• demolish a gate, fence, wall or railing over 1m high next to a highway or public open space or over 2m high elsewhere.

Also if you intend to cut down or lop any tree within a conservation area you are required to give six weeks' notice to do so (other than a tree already protected under a Tree Preservation Order – *see* below). This gives the local authority time to apply for a Tree Preservation Order should they so wish. You should contact your local authority to check whether or not the building is in a conservation area and to ascertain whether there are any restrictions such as having to use local materials, for example stone or slate, or any other restrictions peculiar to the area, such as

National Parks and Areas of Outstanding Natural Beauty.

Trees

Many trees have been protected by Tree Preservation Orders (TPOs), which means that consent is needed from the local authority to lop, prune or fell them. However, a TPO cannot prohibit the uprooting, lopping or felling of a tree that is dying or is indeed dead and has become dangerous. If a landowner fells a protected tree without permission, the local authority has the powers to insist that a replacement tree of a suitable size is planted at his or her expense.

Rights of Way

Should your proposals require the alteration or obstruction of a public path that crosses the property, you should contact the local authority at a very early stage.

A footpath post or sign is the first indication of a right of way. An Ordnance Survey map of at least 1:50,000 will show the exact route. (Nigel Rigden)

Planning permission itself does not confer any rights to interfere, move or obstruct a public path. In order to do so, you will need to request that the local authority make an Order to divert or close it. The Order must be advertised for a period and anyone is free to object. You cannot obstruct the path until any objections have been heard and the Order has been confirmed.

Wildlife

Some buildings will contain bats, owls and other protected species of wildlife. The Wildlife and Countryside Act 1981 gives special protection to bats when carrying out any works that are likely to disturb them, for example timber treatment, demolitions or building alterations.

Bats in England and Wales are also protected by the additions to the Wildlife and Countryside Act, which are embodied in the Countryside and Rights of Way Act 2000; this does not apply to Scotland or Northern Ireland or Eire. Bats across the European Union are protected by the Habitats Directive, which has been put into British law in the Habitats Regulations 1994. Therefore you are legally obliged to seek advice from your local Statutory Nature Conservation Organization (SNCO) if you plan to undertake any work in or around a bat roost. These SNCOs are English Nature, Scottish Natural Heritage, the Countryside Council for Wales and the Environment and Heritage Service (Northern Ireland). They will then advise on the best course of action, particularly with regard to breeding seasons.

The Bat Conservation Trust and its volunteer workers have been particularly instrumental in carrying out research into the effect on bats when properties that contain bat roosts are converted. One of the BCT's leaflets is reproduced here.

It is also common for planning permissions to contain conditions regarding the preservation of wildlife that require you to carry out a wildlife survey prior to any works being undertaken. You will also be required to demonstrate how you intend to protect any species of wildlife found, for example house martins and badgers, and you will certainly need the advice of a professional ecological consultant in difficult cases.

BUILDING REGULATIONS

The Building Act 1984 provides the legal framework for the Building Regulations 2000 in England and Wales. In Scotland it is the Building (Scotland) Act for 1959/1970 for the Building Standards (Scotland) Regulations 1990, as amended. The Scottish Regulations are in essence the same but for the procedures connected with 'Building Warrants'. One is required before commencement of work, and under the procedure there is a requirement for you to obtain a 'Certificate of Completion' prior to occupation of the building.

The Regulations are statutory instruments, which have been imposed by Government to deal with the minimum standards of design and building work and state clearly what is regarded as building work and set out the procedures for ensuring that the minimum requirements are met.

These are separate and in addition to any requirements imposed under the Planning Acts. Building work, which is not necessarily subject to planning approval, may well require Building Regulation Approval. You should in any case contact your local authority Building Control officer to ascertain what is required. Also, unless you have a reasonable knowledge of building construction it would be advisable to obtain professional advice (see Chapter 4). There are financial penalties for contravening the Regulations and for building without notification. Also you can be asked to demolish any works not in compliance; if you fail to do so, the local authority has the powers to demolish the work and recover the costs from yourself!

The Regulations contain a list of requirements contained in Schedule 1, which are specifically designed to:

- ensure the health, safety, welfare and convenience of persons in or around buildings
- provide for the conservation of fuel and power
- prevent waste, undue consumption, misuse or contamination of water
- provide access and facilities for disabled persons.

The Office of the Deputy Prime Minister produces a free explanatory booklet entitled *Building Regulations*, which is a comprehensive guide to the act and how it is applied and what you need to know and do.

FOLLOWING PAGES: Bats and Buildings in the UK *is a very useful leaflet produced by the Bat Conservation Trust.* (The Bat Conservation Trust)

45

PROFESSIONAL SUPPORT SERIES

BATS AND BUILDINGS IN THE UK

Increasingly bats use buildings for roosting, as natural roosting places in tree holes and caves become more scarce or disturbed. All buildings, in particular the walls, eaves and roofs, are potential roost sites.

Anyone working regularly in these areas, such as surveyors, architects, plumbers, roofers, pest technicians, double glazing installers and insulators, should be aware of what signs to look for.
(The information provided here is believed to be correct. However, no responsibility can be accepted by the Bat Conservation Trust or any of its partners or officers for any consequences of errors or omissions, nor responsibility for loss occasioned to any person acting or refraining from action as a result of this information and no claims for compensation for damage or negligence will be accepted)

LEGAL PROTECTION

All 16 species of UK bat are protected by law. This differs slightly from country to country, but in summary it is illegal to:

> **kill, injure or disturb bats**
> **obstruct access to bat roost**
> **damage or disturb bat roosts**

because of the following legislation:-
- Wildlife and Countryside Act 1981 (covers England, Scotland and Wales). Northern Ireland bats are protected by the Wildlife (Northern Ireland) Order 1985. The Wildlife Act 1990 is relevant for the Isle of Man.
- Countryside and Rights of Way (CROW) Act 2000 (covers England and Wales).
- The Habitats Directive (Council Directive 92/43/EEC) on the Conservation of Natural Habitats and of Wild Fauna and Flora.

In this context 'damage' would include such operations as treatment with chemicals found in wood preservatives. 'Disturbance' includes any work in or affecting a bat roost.

Under the law, a roost is any structure or place used by bats for shelter or protection. Because bats tend to re-use the same roosts year after year, the roost is protected whether or not bats are present at the time.

In order that legislation is not contravened, any building, maintenance, or other operation needing to be carried out where there are bats or evidence of bats must be notified to the relevant Statutory Nature Conservation Organisation (SNCO) or government department in order that it can advise on whether the operation should be carried out and, if so, the method to be used and the timing.

Where works likely to affect bats and/or roosts are proposed for a house, your SNCO (EN, SNH, CCW or Environment & Heritage Service NI) needs to be informed in order to advise on how you should proceed.

Where works affect other buildings or structures e.g. tree or bridge works/maintenance, any demolition (including houses), building maintenance, barn conversions, works to churches etc, then the appropriate Government department (i.e. DEFRA, Welsh Assembly, Scottish Executive, Environment & Heritage Service NI) needs to be informed and a Habitats Regulations Licence application submitted to and approved by them before any work can commence. Procedures for this can be quite lengthy, so bat surveys should be undertaken as early as possible in the proceedings. *In all cases, a timely survey by an experienced bat worker can save delays later.*

WHERE do bats roost in buildings?

Different species of bats prefer different places; some creep into tiny spaces, cracks and crevices. Only occasionally do they hang free, or are easily visible.

Outside they may roost:
- under weather boarding or hanging tiles
- above soffits and behind fascia and barge boarding
- between window frame and wall brickwork
- in gaps behind cladding tiles or wood
- between underfelt and boards or tiles
- inside cavity walls

brown long-eared bat

Inside roof spaces they may roost:
- along the ridge beam
- around the gable end
- around the chimney breast

LOOKING for the evidence

Bats do not make nests or cause structural damage. The most obvious sign of their presence is droppings.
- Bat droppings consist largely of insect remains and crumble easily between your fingers to a powder of semi-shiny fragments.
- Rodent droppings are smooth and plastic, quickly becoming hard. They cannot be crumbled.
- Bat droppings do not present any known health hazards.
- Droppings may not always be readily visible in a loft.
- Large accumulations may reflect use over a number of years rather than large numbers of bats at any one time.

Bat droppings are frequently mistaken for mouse droppings, so do the 'crumble test'.

© The Bat Conservation Trust   Reg. Charity no 1012361 Company limited by guarantee, registered in England no 2712823

WHEN do bats use buildings?

Bats use buildings at any time, but are most often found in houses between May and August.

- Mother bats have only one baby a year, suckling it for several weeks. The mothers gather in maternity roosts to have their babies in summer, and this is the time they are most likely to be seen using buildings.
- The bats move away when the young can fly and feed themselves, and have usually left by September.
- Immature individuals, adult males and non-breeding females will occupy a variety of roosts, individually or in small groups, at any time of year.
- Disturbance or the use of chemicals at maternity roosts in houses can have a major impact on bat populations gathered from a wide area.
- Bats do roost in houses in winter, usually individually, but are difficult to see.

WHICH bats use buildings?

All our UK species have been recorded in houses, but some very rarely. Pipistrelle and long-eared bats are the species most usually found.

Pipistrelle bat

Pipistrelle bats: Only recently have scientists recognised that there are three species of pipistrelle in the UK.

They sometimes use houses as maternity roosts, choosing confined spaces. These are usually on the outside of the buildings, such as under soffits or behind barge boards or hanging tiles, where the bats can rarely be seen.

Brown long-eared bat: This animal mostly prefers older houses with large roof spaces. Small clusters may be seen at junctions of roof timbers or under the ridge. It is the bat most frequently seen inside lofts, and small numbers may stay longer than other species.

BEST PRACTICE
for working in bat roosts

- In order to work within the law, seek advice from the appropriate Statutory Nature Conservation Organisation (SNCO) in any situation where an operation may affect bats or their roosts (see *Contacts* below).
- If operations have already started when bats or their roosts are discovered, work must stop and the relevant SNCO be contacted immediately.

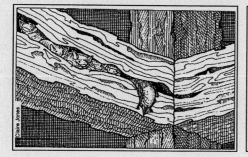

PEST CONTROL
in a bat roost

The control of pests such as wasps, bees, hornets, cluster flies and rodents may unintentionally affect bats or their roosts, so care should be taken when controlling pests in an area where bats are, or are known to have been, present.

- Rodenticides should not be placed in an open tray below roosting bats.
- Insecticides recommended as safer for use near mammals are based on boron, permethrin or cypermethrin. Obtain details from SNCOs.
- Ask for advice too on the range of fungicides which may be used in sites used by bats.
- Sticky traps should not be used in bat roosts.

Advice must be sought from your SNCO before any action is taken in order to keep within the Law.

CONTACTS

The Headquarters of the Statutory Nature Conservation Organisations (SNCOs) are:

English Nature (EN),
Northminster House,
Peterborough PE1 1UA
Tel: 01733 455000
www.english-nature.org.uk

Countryside Council for Wales (CCW),
Plas Penrhos, Fford Penrhos, Bangor,
Gwynedd LL57 2LQ.
Tel: 01248 385500
www.ccw.gov.uk

Scottish Natural Heritage (SNH),
12 Hope Terrace,
Edinburgh EH9 2AS
Tel: 0131 447 4784
www.snh.org.uk

Environment & Heritage Service,
Commonwealth House, 35 Castle Street, Belfast,
N.Ireland BT1 1GH.
Tel: 02890 546558

When a Habitats Regulations licence is required you need to contact your government department. Your SNCO will be able to advise of its address.

The Bat Conservation Trust
15 Cloisters House
8 Battersea Park Road
London SW8 4BG

Tel: 0845 1300 228
Email: enquiries@bats.org.uk
Web site: www.bats.org.uk

The Bat Conservation Trust is the only national organisation solely devoted to the conservation of bats and their habitats. Write for an information pack and membership details.

October 2002

Cover of Building Regulations Explanatory Booklet. (HMSO)

Building Regulations – Approved Documents

The parts to Schedule 1 and Regulation 7 are supported by separate documents called 'Approved Documents', which give practical and technical guidance on how the various requirements can be met. Copies of these can be purchased from Her Majesty's Stationery Office or can be downloaded from the Internet (if you have the patience!).

There are thirteen parts (A to N – there is as yet no Part I) to Schedule 1, which cover:

A. Structure

Buildings are to be constructed so that all loads are transmitted to the ground safely and without any distortion to any part of the building or the ground on which it stands. The building is to be constructed so that its stability is not affected by subsidence, shrinkage, swelling or freezing of the subsoil. If a building is of five storeys or more, for example a warehouse, there is a requirement that its construction will be such that it will not suffer collapse disproportionate to the cause. The next revision of the rule will take into account the events of 11 September 2001 in New York and will need to consider terrorist attack.

B. Fire Safety

Buildings are to be constructed so that there is a satisfactory means of raising the alarm and of escape in the event of a fire and to enable access for fire appliances. It is also necessary to inhibit the spread of fire to internal linings and the external envelope and ensure stability of buildings in a fire. There must be a sufficient degree of fire-separating structure within buildings and between those adjoining.

C. Site Preparation and Resistance to Moisture

The ground upon which any building is to stand should be free of vegetable matter and precautions should be taken to avoid health and safety issues caused by any dangerous or offensive substances found on or below the ground. The ground should be drained and the walls, floors and roof of the building should resist the passage of moisture to the inside.

Part C is currently being rewritten with Regulation 6, to take into account conversions of agricultural and industrial property in respect of likely contamination and the need to deal with this adequately. Also, resistance to contaminants will be expanded to include the whole of the site, extra remedial measures and more advice on radon. The provisions for subsoil drainage are to be widened to take into account rising ground water and flooding, as well as the effects of water-borne contaminants. The new Part C will for the first time take into account climate change and will include Regulations to deal with the increased frequency and severity of driving rain.

D. Toxic Substances

If insulating materials are inserted into a cavity wall reasonable precautions are to be taken to prevent any toxic fumes permeating to any part of the building.

E. Resistance to the Passage of Sound

Any wall that separates one dwelling from another shall resist the passage of sound; also any wall that separates a habitable room from any other part of the same building, which is not part of the same dwelling. Any floor or stair separating one dwelling from another shall resist airborne or impact sound; also any floor or stair that separates a habitable room from any other part of the same building, which is not part of the same dwelling. This document has recently been extensively revised to bring in much higher standards for noise attenuation between habitable rooms and between dwellings. There is also a requirement for site testing. This is an attempt to deal with the nuisance caused by high-powered audio systems and the reverberation set up by them.

F. Ventilation

There should be adequate ventilation for occupants of a building unless the space is used as a store or garage. Also adequate provision should be made to prevent excessive condensation in roofs and roof voids. With the latest revisions to Part L1 (*see below*), there will be a change to more controlled ventilation in order to conserve energy.

G. Hygiene

Adequate sanitary conveniences and washing facilities are to be provided. These are to be separated from places where food is prepared, and suitable provision is to be made for hot and cold water to washbasins, showers and baths. A bathroom shall be provided which contains either a bath or fixed shower. If hot-water storage systems are not vented, they are to be installed by a competent person.

H. Drainage and Waste Disposal

A system of drainage shall be provided to carry wastewater from any sanitary appliance to a public or private sewer, septic tank or cesspit. Rainwater from roofs and paved areas should discharge into an adequate soakaway, sewer or watercourse. There are specific regulations on the construction of septic tanks, drainage fields and reed beds, recycled waste storage and pumping systems. There are provisions for protection from rats and alterations to existing sewers.

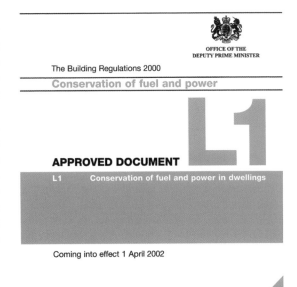

Cover of Approved Document L1 *for conservation of fuel and power.* (HMSO)

J. Combustion Appliances and Fuel Storage Systems

Combustion appliances should be installed with an adequate air supply and with provision for discharge of combustion products to the outside air. Combustion appliances should be installed to avoid injury to people and risks of the building catching fire. Hearths, fireplaces or chimneys should have information provided on their performance and be fixed to the building to allow safe installation of any combustion appliance. Liquid-fuel storage systems should be sited and constructed so as to avoid fire to adjacent buildings. Oil-storage systems should be sited and constructed to avoid pollution due to oil spillage and leakage.

K. Protection from Falling, Collision and Impact

Stairs, ladders and ramps should be so constructed as

to be safe for people moving from one level to another in or about a building. Barriers should be installed to stop people falling, including from a balcony, or into a light well or sunken area. Provision should be made also to prevent people colliding with open windows, skylights and doors that can be pushed open from both sides.

L. Conservation of Fuel and Power
(There are two parts to this document, L1 and L2. Only L1 deals with dwellings.)

Reasonable provision should be made for the conservation of fuel and power through the fabric of the building, from hot-water pipes, hot-air ducts and hot-water vessels. Also provision should be made for providing space-heating systems and lighting systems, with appropriate lamps and controls, and which are energy efficient. There are rules governing the replacement of existing heating systems and existing windows and doors. There is a specific requirement to provide instructions to users of buildings on the operation of heating systems. There is specific advice on the application of the Regulations to conservation and restoration work to historic buildings. The document details the insulation values required to elements of the building structure, including extensions and conservatories, and requirements to minimize draughts. These values have been greatly uprated to reduce carbon emissions in direct response to the articles agreed in the Kyoto Protocol on climate change.

M. Access and Facilities for Disabled People
Reasonable provision should be made for disabled people to gain access to and be able to use a building unimpeded.

N. Glazing: Safety in Relation to Impact, Opening and Cleaning
Any glazing should break in such a way that it is unlikely to cause injury and be able to resist impact without breaking or be shielded from impact.

Regulation 7. Materials and Workmanship
Building work should be carried out with adequate and proper materials in a workmanlike manner.

What is Covered by the Regulations?
Building works are clearly defined in Regulation 3. Generally the Regulations apply if you put up a new building, extend or alter an existing one, or provide fittings within a building, for example drains or heat-producing appliances. The Regulations will apply to certain changes of use even if no construction work is intended. There is a material change of use where there is a change in the purposes or the circumstances whereby a building is used, for example if after the change a building is used as a dwelling, where previously it was not, or if the building now contains a flat, where previously it did not.

Application for Building Regulations Approval
There are two methods for making an application to the local authority:

- deposit of Full Plans or
- the giving of a Building Notice.

In the Full Plans procedure you will be required to submit a set of drawings showing the existing arrangements and what is proposed, including constructional details. You may also be required to submit structural calculations for load-bearing elements such as beams. This is best left to a competent person (see Chapter 4). There is an application fee to be paid (the plan charge), the amount of which is set according to the type of work. Exemptions to these charges can apply if the works are solely for the use of a disabled person. Once the application has been made the local authority will check the details thoroughly and when these satisfy the Regulations, then between five and eight weeks after deposit an Approval Notice is issued. This allows you to proceed with the works, though you are still required to give a Commencement Notice prior to starting. Payment of an inspection charge is required after the first site visit by the building inspector, and the local authority will then arrange to continue inspecting the work as it proceeds.

Under the Building Notice procedure no approval is given. The advantage, however, is that you are able to commence the work once the Building Notice has been submitted; also you have no requirement to prepare Full Plans. There is still a charge for submitting a Building Notice (a building notice charge), which is equivalent to the total of the application and inspection fees under the Full Plans procedure. To take this route you must be extremely confident that your proposals meet the Regulations. The local authority will arrange to inspect the work as it proceeds to check compliance, but there is a constant risk that any works carried out which are not in accordance with the Regulations will need to be rectified. There is also an obligation to supply further information, for example structural design calculations, prior to undertaking certain sections of the work.

Should your proposals be rejected under the Full Plans procedure or you feel the conditions imposed by the local authority are onerous, then you have the right to appeal to the Secretary of State. You can also seek relaxation or exemption from certain of the Regulations if you believe they do not apply or would conflict with other regulations, for example historic and listed buildings.

THE PARTY WALL ACT

The Party Wall Act 1996 provides a framework for preventing and resolving disputes in relation to party walls, boundary walls and for excavations near neighbouring buildings. It is entirely separate from Planning and Building Regulations controls. The Act covers the following:

- works that are going to be carried out directly to an existing wall or structure shared with another property
- building a wall of a new building or free-standing wall at or astride the boundary line with a neighbouring property
- excavating near a neighbouring building.

If any of your proposals are likely to come within these categories then it is a requirement under the Act that you notify all affected neighbours.

Rights

You have certain rights under the Act, as follows:

- you can cut into the party wall to allow for the bearing of a beam or to insert a damp-proof course through it
- you can raise the whole of the wall
- you can demolish and rebuild the party wall
- you are allowed to underpin the wall
- you are allowed to protect two adjoining walls by installing a flashing from the higher to the lower.

Duties

If you propose to carry out any of the works mentioned above then you must inform all adjoining owners before doing so. It is always preferable to discuss any proposed work with your neighbour(s) and resolve any points of difference. However, you must always give notice in writing about your intentions, which must be done at least two months prior to the commencement date.

Reaching Agreement

The person receiving the notice may give his or her consent in writing or give a counter-notice detailing what changes he or she requires to the proposals. This should be done within fourteen days of receiving the notice; if not, a dispute is regarded to have arisen. Also if you receive a counter-notice you must respond within fourteen days; if not, then again a dispute is said to have arisen.

If you and your neighbour(s) cannot reach agreement, the next thing to do is to appoint, jointly, a surveyor (under the Act an 'Agreed Surveyor' – someone who is completely independent to either party) to draw up an 'award'. This is a document which sets out the works that will be carried out and says when and how the works are to be carried out. It also records the condition of the adjoining property prior to the works and allows access for the surveyor to inspect the works whilst in progress. You will, as the person planning the works, normally have to pay the surveyor's fees for drawing up the award and carrying out inspections.

Building on the Boundary Line

If you intend to build a new party wall on the boundary line, then you should inform your neighbour(s) whether or not you intend to build it up to the line or astride it. You should serve notice on your

SOUTH SOMERSET DISTRICT COUNCIL

FULL PLANS SUBMISSION

The Building Act 1984
The Building Regulations 1991

B.Regs Plan No:

This form is to be filled in by the person who intends to carry out building work or agent. If the form is unfamiliar please read the attached notes or consult the office indicated above. Please type or use block capitals.

1	**Applicant's details** Name: Address: Postcode: Tel: Fax:
2	**Agent's details:** (if applicable) Name: Address: Postcode: Tel: Fax:
3	**LOCATION of Building to which work relates** Address: Postcode: Tel: Fax:
4	**Proposed work** Number of storeys: Description: Date of Commencement (if known)
5	**Use of Building** 1 If new building or extension please state proposed use: 2 If existing building state present use: 3 Is the building to be put, or intended to be put, to a use which is designated under the Fire Precautions Act 1971 **YES/NO**
6	**Additional Information** (a) What is the source of the water supply? Mains ☐ Private ☐ (Please specify) Mode of drainage: (a) Foul Water: Public sewer ☐ Septic Tank ☐ Cesspool ☐ Other (Please specify) (b) Surface Water: Public Sewer ☐ Soakaway ☐ Watercourse Other (Please specify) Have you applied for Town and Country Planning Approval: **YES/NO** - Application No: .... see note G
7	**Completion Certificate** Do you require a completion certificate following satisfactory completion of the building work? **YES/NO**
8	**Statement** This notice is given in relation to the building work as described, and is submitted in accordance with Regulation 11 (1) (b) and is accompanied by the appropriate charge. I understand that further charges will be payable following the first inspection by the local authority. Name: Signature: Date:

**BUILDING REGULATIONS 1991 - CHARGES FOR BUILDING CONTROL
THE BUILDING (LOCAL AUTHORITY CHARGES) REGULATIONS 1998**

Number of Dwellings [   ]   Floor Area of Extension(s) [m²]

	Plan Charge £	Inspection Charge £	Total Schedule 1 Charges
Schedule 1 Charges	[ ]	[ ]	£

			Total Schedule 2 Charges
Schedule 2 Charges	[ ]	[ ]	£
	[ ]	[ ]	£

Total Estimated Cost of Work not covered by Schedule 1 or 2 *(Exclusive of VAT)* [£   ]

			Total Schedule 3 Charges
Schedule 3 Charges	[ ]	[ ]	[ ]

I attach total charge of *(see Note 1)* [£   ]

VAT Receipt required   YES/NO
(Please circle your choice)

Exemption from these charges is allowed for work to provide access and facilities for disabled people.

I / We claim exemption from these charges due to

I / We agree to the prescribed period of five weeks being extended to a maximum of 2 months *(Delete if not applicable)*

NOTE 1   When submitting a Full Plans application the plan charges for Schedule 1 and 2 work need only be paid on submission and 25% of the total charge from Schedule 3 where estimated costs exceed £5,000. Where estimated costs are £5,000 or less the total Schedule 3 charge is payable on deposit and no further inspection charges will be invoiced. Inspection charges including remaining 75% of total charge from Schedule 3 where estimated cost exceed £5,000 will be invoiced on commencement.

NOTE 2   If the Council considers the estimated cost to be an unreasonable one the application will not be accepted.

NOTE 3   The estimated cost for Schedule 3 charges should exclude the cost of work covered by Schedule 1 and 2 charges.

NOTE 4   Charges for dwellings with a floor area exceeding 300m² when excluding garages or carports should be calculated under Schedule 3 method.

NOTE 5   Where an extension to a dwelling, the total floor area of which exceeds 60m² , including means of access and work in connection with that extension the sum of the plan charge and the inspection charge or the building notice charge must not be less than **£521.70.**

NOTE 6   Where an extension or alteration to a dwelling consists of the provision of one or more rooms in a roof space, the sum of the plan charge and the inspection charge or the building notice charge must not be less than **£391.27.**

FOR OFFICE USE ONLY			
Submission Charge checked by	[ ]	Date [ ]	Paid by CHEQUE / CASH

Building Regulations application forms for submission of Full Plans. The application comes with a schedule to enable charges to be calculated for different values of construction cost.
(South Somerset District Council)

Party Walls

There are two types of party wall:

- party wall
- party fence wall

Party Wall

A wall is deemed to be a party wall if it forms part of a building and stands astride the boundary of land belonging to two or more adjoining owners.

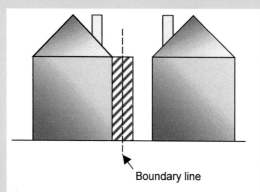

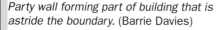
Boundary line

Party wall forming part of building that is astride the boundary. (Barrie Davies)

A wall is also deemed to be a party wall if it separates buildings and it stands either astride the boundary of land or two or more owners.

In addition, it is a party wall if it stands wholly on one of the owner's land but is used by an adjoining owner to separate their buildings. (In the situation that one person has built the wall in the first place, and another has built up to it without actually constructing their own wall, then only part of the wall that does the separating is deemed to be 'party').

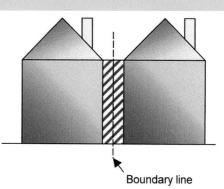
Boundary line

Party wall astride the boundary and separating two buildings. (Barrie Davies)

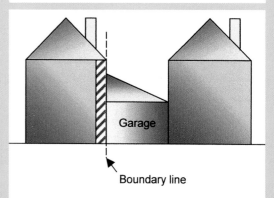
Garage
Boundary line

Party wall on one person's land used by adjoining owner. (Barrie Davies)

Party Fence Wall

A party fence wall is part of a building that stands astride the boundary between the property of different owners and is used to separate them.

neighbour(s) at least one month prior to the works commencing. If agreement is not reached then you must, jointly, appoint a surveyor as before to make an award.

If agreement was reached to build astride the boundary, then the cost of the work would be shared if benefits of the wall were shared. There is no right under the Act to build astride the boundary and if there is no response from your neighbour, then your only option is to build up to the boundary.

CONSTRUCTION (DESIGN AND MANAGEMENT) REGULATIONS

The Construction (Design and Management) Regulations 1994, known as the CDM Regulations, provide the framework for managing health and safety during the construction, repair, maintenance and demolition of building works. The Regulations placed new duties on clients, designers and contractors.

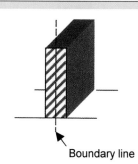

Party fence wall (not part of a building).
(Barrie Davies)

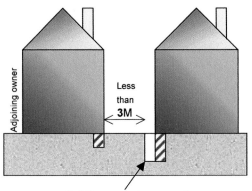

Excavation within 3m of adjoining owner's
building. (Barrie Davies)

(This does not include such things as wooden
fences.)

Excavation Near Neighbouring Buildings
You must inform your neighbour if you intend to:

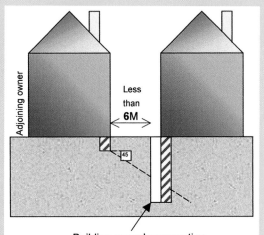

Excavation within 6m of adjoining owner's
building. (Barrie Davies)

- excavate or construct foundations within 3m of
  a neighbouring building he or she owns where
  the work will go deeper than the foundations of
  the building
- excavate or construct foundations within 6m of
  a neighbouring building he or she owns that will
  cut a line drawn at 45° from the bottom of the
  building's foundations.

You should serve notice in writing, stating in particular how you intend to safeguard the building's
foundations. If there is no response or agreement
from your neighbour then a dispute is deemed
to have arisen. This, as mentioned earlier, is
resolved by jointly appointing a party wall surveyor
to make an award under the Party Wall Act.

These regulations do *not* normally apply if the
work is carried out on residential property, though
there is a duty to notify the HSE (Health & Safety
Executive) under Regulation 7 if the works are
expected to take longer than 30 days or 500 person
days. (A person day is counted as one person working
a normal shift.) This is usually done by the contractor
or architect by completing Form 10.

However, the Regulations apply to you in their
entirety if a developer is carrying out the works and

you are intending to purchase the uncompleted
property. The CDM regulations apply also if you are
carrying out the work in the name of a trading
company.

The Regulations *always* apply to professional
designers, whether the property is for residential use
or not. They have a duty to ensure that any design
avoids and combats foreseeable risks to the health
and safety of anyone carrying out construction or
cleaning work. The designer must also ensure that

the design includes adequate information about any aspect of the project that might affect the health or safety of any person at work carrying out construction or cleaning work in or on the structure.

Useful Information and Contacts

Government publications from the Internet

1. **Planning**
   - General: *www.planning.odpm.gov.uk*
   - *Planning – A Guide for Householders: www.planning.odpm.gov.uk/householders/guide*

2. **Construction Legislation**
   - General: *www.safety.odpm.gov.uk/bregs/index*
   - *Building Regulations Explanatory Booklet: www.safety.odpm.gov.uk/bregs/brpub/br-booklet/whole*
   - *Building Regulations – Approved Documents: www.safety.odpm.gov.uk/bregs/brads*
   - *Building Regulations – Guide to Determinations and Appeals: www.safety.odpm.gov.uk/bregs/app-det*
   - *Party Wall Act Explanatory Booklet: www.safety.odpm.gov.uk/bregs/pwact/index*

3. **Regional Matters**
   - Northern Ireland: *www.ni-assembly.gov.uk*
   - Scotland: *www.scotland-legislation.hmso.gov.uk*
   - Wales: *www.wales-legislation.hmso.gov.uk*

4. **Planning Acts & Building Regulations**
   - *www.hmso.gov.uk*

5. **Wildlife**
   - English Nature (EN): Tel. 01733 455000; *www.english-nature.org.uk*
   - Countryside Council for Wales (CCW): Tel. 01248 385500; *www.ccw.gov.uk*
   - Scottish Natural Heritage (SNH): Tel. 0131 447 4784; *www.snh.org.uk*
   - Environment & Heritage Service (Northern Ireland): Tel. 02890 546558; *www.ehsni.gov.uk*

CHAPTER 3

Finance, Budgeting and Taxation

OBTAINING FINANCE

Perhaps you have won the National Lottery or have been left some money in a will. If so, the first part of this chapter will not interest you in the least. For the rest of us, however, obtaining finance is a necessary hurdle to owning property, and it is where one has to go cap – or plans – in hand to the various lenders. It is relatively straightforward to put your case when you are purchasing a new property or one that has already been converted because a market value can readily be put on it. The lender in these circumstances has then some tangible security and can, in the final resort, repossess the property to recoup his costs.

It is a very different matter if the property is derelict and represents little or no security to the lender. He is undoubtedly going to be more cautious and will seek all sorts of assurances apart from the usual guarantees. He has also to be convinced that what is being converted and your proposals will represent an asset that can be readily disposed of should things go wrong.

Searching the high street or Internet for what is known as a 'self build' mortgage will produce mixed results and it may be better to use an adviser, who will be able to contact a panel of lenders prepared to lend to people converting property. In addition, there are companies who specialize in self build packages that include a choice of suitable mortgage from a panel of lenders and appropriate insurance to cover the site works.

It is also possible to take out a short-term loan from a high street bank or building society secured against the equity in your existing property or against the value of the unconverted building and land. This,

commonly known as a bridging loan, is charged at a premium over normal borrowing rates, and is normally repaid upon completion of the works to the new property. This is done by either selling your existing property to release the equity or by transferring the loan into a normal mortgage on the new property. Obviously, in the latter situation, you will be faced with paying mortgages on both your existing and new property if you are unable to sell.

The advantage of this type of loan is that it provides positive cash flow and means you do not have to sell or move out of your existing home to finance the project. A number of lenders are now offering bridging finance tailored to converting property and claim to be more competitive than high street banks and building societies.

The Self-Build Mortgage

This was primarily designed to serve the needs of people building a new home on a greenfield site using their own or subcontracted labour. However, such mortgages are also appropriate for people converting property, whether they are carrying out the work themselves or employing a builder.

The significant difference between a self-build mortgage and a normal house purchase mortgage is that the money is released in stages relating to the build progress as opposed to all the money being available up front. You can normally borrow up to 95 per cent of the purchase price and 95 per cent of the conversion costs, although this can vary from lender to lender. However, the appropriate planning permission must be in place before any lender will consider releasing funds.

Typical Stages for Release of Funds	
1. Purchase of the land and property	This is the cost of the land and buildings as agreed with the vendor.
2. Preliminary costs and structural repairs	This will include all fees, e.g. solicitor's fees, structural survey, local authority and preliminary architect's fees. It will also include urgent repairs, demolitions, any foundations and underground drainage and services trenches.
3. Building made wind and watertight	This will include the roof, windows and external doors: possibly also rainwater disposal systems and external drainage. It will also include the floor slabs and repairs and modifications to the structural envelope of the building.
4. Internal works and first fix services	This will include installation of staircases, stud partitions, ceilings, masonry walls and plastering. It will include the first fix electrical, heating and plumbing installations and underfloor heating.
5. Second fix	This will include installations of kitchens, bathrooms, fitted cupboards, internal doors and linings and any joinery. Final service connections are also made. It will also include second fix of electrical fittings, radiators etc.
6. Completion	This will include decorations, floor finishes, landscaping, fences and driveways.

The money is normally released in arrears after inspection by a surveyor appointed by the lender or certified by the architect, if one is appointed. This creates a negative cash flow and you will need to ensure that you have sufficient liquid funds available for the purchase of materials and labour or be in a position to pay the contractor's interim invoices.

Some lenders have brought out what they call 'accelerator' self-build mortgages. Here the funds are released in *advance* of each building stage and no inspections or interim valuations are made. These have the advantage that funds are available prior to any of the work being carried out and before bills have to be paid. Some of these schemes have

bridging-loan type arrangements added on, which, as highlighted earlier, mean you would not have to sell your home to fund the purchase of the building or the cost of the works.

Self-build mortgages are available in as many types as are found for normal home mortgages. There are so many variations and each has its advantages and disadvantages depending on your circumstances and the rise and fall of the bank rate. The market is continually being showered with new products to fill niche situations but they are generally based on the same principles. You should contact the various lenders for the latest products, but the commonly available types are listed below:

- **Capped Rate** This type of mortgage puts a ceiling on interest rate rises on the prevailing rate for an agreed period but gives the benefit of any reduction in rates.
- **Discounted** This mortgage gives a discount on the lender's normal variable rate for a set period. This allows for lower interest payments in the early years of the mortgage. At the end of the period the mortgage reverts to the lender's normal variable rate.
- **Fixed** The mortgage interest rate is fixed for a number of years and is independent of general interest rate changes. The fixed period is usually between two and seven years, though the longer the period the higher the rate charged at the outset. This type of mortgage enables monthly outgoings to be planned with certainty over a number of years. At the end of the fixed period, the mortgage reverts to the lender's normal variable rate.
- **Flexible** These mortgages allow over- and underpayment or the taking of a 'holiday'. Any overpayment reduces the outstanding mortgage and any underpayment is added to the amount owed.
- **Self-certification** This is an appropriate mortgage for the self-employed or a contractor with difficulty in proving an income.
- **Tracker** This mortgage tracks the Bank of England base rate by a set percentage.
- **Variable** This is the normal mortgage product and as the name suggests it goes up and down in line with changes in the base rate.

How Much Can be Borrowed?

There are loans of 100 per cent available, but commonly the maximum is 95 per cent with the borrower finding a deposit of 5 per cent. Money is normally lent as follows:

- If two persons are borrowing together the banks and building societies will normally lend: up to three times the first annual income plus one times the second; or two and a half times the joint income before tax
- If a single individual is borrowing, then three times the annual income before tax can be offered.

- If a person is self-employed then an average of the last three years' income can be taken into account, with the above multipliers being applied.

These above figures are only indicative and can vary from lender to lender.

Applying for a Mortgage

To apply for a mortgage you will have to provide a number of recent payslips and your latest P60 in order to prove your income. If you are self-employed then a few years' audited accounts will be required. In addition, those who are proposing to carry out a conversion will need to submit the plans and specifications to the lender along with evidence of the relevant planning approval.

PURCHASE

Once you have found the property, even if it is not for sale (as is often the case with a lot of derelict property), a price must be agreed with the vendor and an offer made. Valuing a property is difficult and a local estate agent might be able to help. Unfortunately, no two properties are alike and do not have the same potential.

This offer usually will be conditional on planning permission being granted for conversion to residential use. If the offer is acceptable then solicitors are usually appointed to carry out all the legal work, make searches to the local authority regarding development plans for the area. They will also contact statutory undertakers to ascertain where electrical, gas, telephone and drainage utilities are located and connected. The solicitor will also check boundaries and whether or not there are any existing planning consents or restrictions. You will certainly need to have a survey carried out to ascertain the condition of the structure, what can be safely left and what will need to be repaired, renewed or demolished (*see* Chapter 1).

If all turns out as planned and there are no surprises, then you will need to consider how much the project is going to cost. You already know the purchase price, have an idea of what your solicitor is going to charge and have probably already paid for the survey. However, at this point you know only in

This barn still has its roof and window and has huge potential. (Barrie Davies)

general terms what you are going to do to the property and possibly are not yet certain whether all your ideas can be fulfilled. If you need to borrow to finance the project, then before making an application you will certainly need to know how much money you will require to carry out the proposed works. To do this effectively you will need a rough scheme and costing. This all has to be carried out quite quickly, in case someone else is also interested in the property and you risk losing it to them.

Estimating

It is relatively straightforward to estimate the cost of building a new house as there are published tables giving the price per square metre. For conversions, there is no guide, as every project is different and the condition of the original property is infinitely variable. However, as a very rough rule you could estimate that conversion would cost anything between £700 and £1,000 per square metre (excluding service connections).

There are pricing books that give rates for the various elements of the building, for example roofing, drainage and so on. However, unless you know the areas and quantities involved these books are not much use. There are rule of thumb percentages which help to gauge the amounts that are normally spent in any section of the work. They are a useful check on the make-up of the estimate and if it does not follow the pattern then you will need to consider the reasons why.

These disused farmyard sheds have little intrinsic value and most of the elements, for example the roofs, will need to be replaced. (Nigel Rigden)

Estimates of Building Works in Property Conversions	
Element	**Between**
Building work	60% and 75%
Services and drainage*	15% and 25%
External works	5% and 10%
The total cost can be further broken down into:	
• labour	35%
• materials	65%

* Depending on cost of service connections.

You can, of course, ask a local builder to price the works, but you will need some sort of schedule for the works proposed. The best course of action, and the simplest, is to employ a professional who can produce a sketch scheme and prepare a rough estimate (*see* Chapter 4).

Once you have your estimate be sure it includes all the works proposed, such as demolition, drainage and external works. For items that could not be given a realistic estimate you will need provisional sums to cover them. A building-cost contingency should also be allowed for items that could not be foreseen prior to starting work on site. If anything has been omitted or forgotten at the planning stage, you will only have the contingency to fall back on. The contingency should therefore be sufficient to cover omissions, but not so large as to jeopardize your borrowing limit. A contingency of between 5 per cent and 10 per cent is usually sufficient, although if the site and buildings have had a poor survey report then a higher figure may need to be considered. However, it is always best practice to get estimates for items covered in the report rather than rely heavily on the contingency.

BUDGETING

Before you borrow, you will need to know all the likely costs involved in the project in addition to the purchase price and estimate of the conversion works.

These additional costs, which whilst not as significant as the purchase and build costs, nevertheless raise the cost of the overall project considerably. These are often overlooked in the budgeting process, especially as some of the costs may have already been incurred, for example architect, solicitor and engineer fees.

Legal Fees These are payable to your solicitor and include conveyancing, Land Registry fees and local searches.

Stamp Duty This is levied on the purchase price of properties and land in excess of £60,000. It is at the rate of 1 per cent on values between £60,001 and £250,000, 3 per cent on values between £250,001 and £500,000 and 4 per cent thereafter.

Valuation and Arrangement Fees This is a fee to cover the lender appointing a valuer to assess the present and future value of the property. This is optional and sometimes the lender absorbs this cost anyway. The lender may also charge you an arrangement fee for arranging the loan. This varies with each lender, with some not charging at all.

Site Survey Fees A site survey will be carried out by a surveyor, engineer or architect to highlight any problems of a structural nature and assess any remedial works necessary to the property. Your lender will probably insist on this (*see* Chapter 1).

Design Fees If an architect is appointed, then an allowance should be made for the full fee based as a percentage of the final building cost. Typically, architects charge between 7 to 15 per cent, although this is usually negotiable (*see* Chapter 4).

Valuation

It is important to register the open market value of the existing property and site to be purchased. This figure is not always the purchase price, which maybe discounted or inflated to current market conditions. It should be carried out whether you are taking out a loan or not. A valuation in writing maybe useful in the future if a liability to capital gains tax exists e.g. if it is a second home. This valuation should be carried out by a reputable valuer or estate agent and at the same time, an estimated value should be put on property as if it were completed in accordance with your proposals.

A rough comparison can then be made of the notional uplift in value, from the purchase price, of the completed scheme to the total amount of cash expected to be spent on the project.

If the comparison shows that the spend will roughly equate to, or will be less than the forecast in value, then you are in the comfort zone whereby you will most likely be able to recoup your expenditure should you need to sell soon after completing the works. If the opposite is true then you need to seriously consider revising the budget for the spend to bring it more in line with the uplift figure. However, if this is going to be your dream home or final resting place then none of this matters!

Structural Engineer's Fees An engineer will need to provide you with structural calculations for new openings, beams, new floors and so on. These are necessary for inclusion as part of your Building Regulations application (*see* Chapter 4).

Planning Application Fees The fees vary for outline and detailed applications. You will need to check with the local planning department.

Building Regulations Fees These are based on the cost of the proposed work; tables are included on application forms along with a ready reckoner.

Insurance Premiums *See below.*

Service Connection Charges These are the charges levied by the water, electricity, gas and telecom companies for connecting mains services to the building. The total cost is dependent on which services are available and the distance from the nearest main. These charges vary enormously and quotes should be obtained early in the process.

Alternative Accommodation If you need to sell your existing home, then a cost for temporary accommodation must be factored into the budget. The cost obviously is dependent on the length of the build programme and when you can move into the building.

Removal Costs Often forgotten about, these costs can be higher than you think and therefore should be included in the budget.

Getting the budget wrong is an error, regularly made, which usually leads to problems during the works on site, with the strong possibility of running out of funds during the contract and not being able to complete the works properly. Budgeting is therefore a crucial stage that should be given thorough consideration.

INSURANCE

There are a number of insurance policies that need to be taken out during the project. They are designed to cover different risks, and consist of the following.

Mortgage Indemnity Insurance This is an arrangement that covers the lender should the new property be repossessed and the lender be unable to recoup the money lent.

Structural Defects Liability Insurance This is a warranty to cover structural defects that may occur during the construction process, or which may only become apparent some years after completion. The mortgage lender is likely to insist on a warranty. Evidence of such a policy will certainly be required when you sell the property. (This is not to be confused with the normal household insurance.)

Example of a Budget Checklist

Item	Comment	Estimate £
1. Purchase cost	As agreed	75,000
2. Estimate of building works	To include demolitions, remedial works, drainage and external works, including landscaping	125,000
3. Legal fees	Ask for charges at outset	5,000
4. Stamp duty	Above £60,000	150
5. Valuation and arrangement fees	Ask lender if these apply	400
6. Site survey fees	Cost dependent on the site and building and what types of survey are required by the lender	1,000
7. Design fees	Dependent upon services required	12,500
8. Structural engineer's fees	Dependent upon services required	500
9. Planning application fees	Likely to be the change of use application fee	220
10. Building Regulations fees	Sliding scale	750
11. Insurance premiums	Shop around	2,000
12. Service connection charges	Quotes required	2,500
13. Alternative accommodation	Caravan on site or rented accommodation?	2,500
14. Removal costs	Quotes to be obtained	1,000
	Total Budget cost	**228,520**
	(Less equity)	–150,000
	Amount to be borrowed	**78,520**

Site Insurance The policy is one that combines public liability, employer's liability and contract works insurance. This cover needs to be taken out at the same time that the purchase of the property is completed, especially if the building is derelict and there are no secure boundaries. You will then be covered from injury to trespassers and injury to others whilst surveys and preliminary works are being undertaken. You will also be covered for theft and damage to the property. The three elements provide the following cover:

- **Public Liability Insurance** This covers typically up to £2,000,000 with respect to injury to any

63

persons, loss of or damage to property. It also covers obstruction, trespass, nuisance or interference with any right of way, air, light or resulting financial loss.

- **Employer's Liability Insurance** This covers, for example, up to £10,000,000 with respect to injury of employees for which you are legally liable. This covers subcontractors and individuals employed by you.
- **Contract Works Insurance** This covers damage to the building in the course of construction and the materials on site from damage and theft. This cover is provided normally on an 'all risks' basis, for example fire, theft, storm, flood, vandalism, subsidence and impact. You are required to provide a sum that should be sufficient to cover the full reinstatement value of the contract works and the existing structure. The policy can include cover for caravans on site and hired or owned plant.

If you employ a contractor, he will carry his own contract works insurance, but it is better not to rely solely on his policy. It may have exclusions and not suit your requirements, especially if you employ others who may not be insured. You may, in any case, be required under the contract to insure the existing buildings (*see* Chapter 7).

TAXATION

VAT

The building costs of converting property to living accommodation are free of VAT. Similarly the building and land purchased for conversion are free of VAT provided you inform the vendor of the future purpose.

Customs and Excise produces Notice No. 719 entitled *VAT Refunds for Do-It-Yourself Builders and Converters*, which gives guidance on:

- Who is entitled to make VAT claims under the Refund Scheme.
- What construction projects are eligible under the Refund Scheme.
- What VAT can be reclaimed.
- How to make a claim.
- The time limits for making a claim.

Who and What are Eligible You can claim a refund on eligible goods and services that are used to convert a non-residential building into a dwelling provided the works are carried out in the UK (including the Isle of Man but not the Channel Islands). The works must be carried out *lawfully* and the building must not be intended for business purposes, for example bed and breakfast accommodation. If the conversion was carried out speculatively for sale or lease then VAT is not reclaimable.

A non-residential conversion takes place when the building (or part) being converted has never been used as a dwelling(s) or has not been used as a dwelling(s) in the ten years prior to the commencement of the works. This is provided that it is designed as a dwelling and is intended solely for residential purposes. This ten-year rule applies particularly in the cases of public houses with living accommodation and crofts.

Eligible Goods These are generally building materials to be incorporated into the building. You cannot claim for items such as carpets, furniture, garden ornaments, sheds, greenhouses and consumables. You can claim for such things as kitchen units and fitted storage systems that are integral with the building. Notice No. 719 contains a comprehensive list of what is eligible and what is not.

Services You do not need to carry out all the work yourself, but if you use a contractor then he *must* charge a reduced rate of 5 per cent, which can then be reclaimed. The builder's VAT can only be claimed back if he has charged the correct rate, as you cannot reclaim the VAT if he has charged you the normal rate. In general, you cannot claim VAT back on services, for example professional and other consultancy fees.

Making a Claim You will need a claim pack from Customs and Excise and you will need to submit all your invoices and receipts with the claim. You will also need to include a copy of the planning permission and plans of the building. Also to prove completion of the works you will need to send a copy of the Building Regulations completion certificate, although a statement from your lender is acceptable saying that the last instalment of the loan has been released (if stage payments have been made in arrears). The claim will usually be settled within thirty days.

Time Limits The claim must be made not more than three months after the conversion work has finished.

VAT and Listed Buildings

If the structure is listed and the works have been granted Listed Building Consent, the cost of the work to it can be zero-rated by VAT-registered contractors. This only applies to works of alteration and not to repairs and maintenance, which are subject to the 5 per cent rate that then needs to be reclaimed. There is a duty on the contractor to apportion the works between alteration and repairs and maintenance in a fair and reasonable way.

Professional and consultancy services are VAT-rated, in the normal way, and cannot be reclaimed.

Capital Gains Tax

Capital Gains Tax (CGT) is levied on the capital sum produced when you dispose of an asset, such as when you sell something of value. Your principal asset is likely to be your home, but if it is your main residence there is no CGT to pay when you sell it. However, if you remain in your existing home whilst converting the new property and then sell the converted property without occupying it, you will be liable for CGT. You also need to be aware that if you occupy the new property for less than a year and then sell it, you will be considered a property developer and be taxed accordingly. Guidance should be sought from the Inland Revenue and leaflet IR283, which is available online, gives you more detail.

GRANT AID

Housing Grants

The Housing Grants, Construction and Regeneration Act 1996 includes a section on grant aid for converting buildings to one or more dwellings.

Examples of Work to Listed Buildings and How They are Treated for VAT	
Work Element	**VAT Treatment**
Extensions	Alteration*
New openings where one did not exist before	Alteration*
Replacing rotten windows with UPVC double glazing	Repair† or alteration*
Replacement of flat roof with pitched roof	Alteration*
Re-felt and batten roof	Repair† or alteration*
Damp-proofing	Repair† or alteration*
Extending plumbing and wiring systems	Alteration*
Rewiring	Repair† or alteration*
Repointing	Repair† or alteration*

* Alterations – zero-rated.
† Repair or maintenance – VAT-rated.

Conversion of this listed church attracted grant aid from English Heritage to enable the original architectural features to be properly preserved. (Nigel Rigden)

These are known as renovation grants and local housing authorities are responsible for administering them. They are means-tested and you may have had to be in occupation of the property (or part of it) for three years prior to the application. If you sell the property within five years, the money has to be returned. You cannot let out the premises as holiday accommodation and it cannot be a second home. The conversion works must be carried out by a contractor who is able to issue an invoice for the release of the grant monies.

You have to make a conversion application to the local housing authority. It is dependent on the policy of the council and on the financial resources available at the time whether or not the application will be considered. All local authorities have discretion regarding where they spend the money and tend to prioritize areas of need.

Disabled facilities grants are also available for such things as alterations to access arrangements and washing and WC facilities for a disabled occupier. This grant is means-tested.

Historic Buildings

Some Historic Buildings Grants are available from English Heritage for works to listed buildings and churches.

The Environment and Heritage Service does the same for Northern Ireland and Historic Scotland for Scotland. In Wales, Cadw can be contacted to provide information.

Some local authorities are also able to give grants. The Architectural Heritage Fund has a website, which gives a list of sources of funding for England and Wales for historic buildings and has a useful search engine.

Redundant Buildings

Local authorities provide grants for regenerating redundant or unusable buildings for business purposes. These grants may also apply to conversion projects where the intention is to provide serviced tourist accommodation and where there is evidence of demand. Hence, if you are dealing with a group of redundant buildings, and you are intending to live in part and rent the remainder as serviced holiday lets, then you could be eligible for financial assistance. However, you should note that the VAT rules change when you are intending to let property and you will not be able to claim any VAT back.

Useful Information and Contacts

- Self-build mortgages and insurance: *www.buildstore.co.uk*
- Self build mortgages and insurance: *www.selfbuildit.co.uk*
- VAT on non-residential conversions (Notice No. 719) and listed buildings (Notice No. 708): *www.hmce.gov.uk*
- VAT national advice line: Tel. 0845 010 9000
- Inland Revenue: *www.inlandrevenue.gov.uk*

- Housing grants: *www.odpm.gov.uk*
- Architectural Heritage Fund: *www.heritage.co.uk*
- Funds for historic buildings: *www.ffhb.org.uk*
- English Heritage: *www.english-heritage.org.uk*
- Environment and Heritage Service for Northern Ireland: *www.ehsni.gov.uk*
- Historic Scotland: *www.historic-scotland.gov.uk*
- Cadw: *www.cadw.wales.gov.uk*

CHAPTER 4

Professional Help and Advice

THE NEED FOR PROFESSIONAL ADVICE

Home conversions often appeal to people who want to do things themselves. There are many tasks you can do perfectly well yourself, depending on your skills. Perhaps you could do your own conveyancing or check out the soundness of the property. You could possibly make the necessary applications to the local planners and carry out negotiations with them, and perhaps also apply for permission under Building Control. You may be able to prepare all the necessary drawings and specifications, obtain estimates and manage the project day to day. Self-build can be a cheaper way of getting what you want and can be very rewarding. Unfortunately, there can be downsides and at least some professional help will probably be necessary at some stage. It is therefore important to have a clear understanding of what sort of advice is available and to be able to decide when and whether you need to employ professionals. You need to know which are the ones appropriate for the specific task and know how they are appointed and what they will charge.

Going it Alone

It is a good idea before employing any professional to consider what tasks can be managed effectively by yourself. However, you need to be self-critical and realistic! But if you do not intend to employ any professionals you should be aware of some of the pitfalls of going it alone.

A real danger is taking on too much without possessing either the necessary time or skills. You may become very ambitious but lack the appropriate skills to achieve a satisfactory end result. You may perhaps underestimate the commitment required, the multitude of items to deal with, the numerous stages to go through and the level of coordination required. Therefore, unless you have all the necessary skills, commitment and time, you will be far better off employing a professional to look after the project on your behalf. You will, of course, have to pay for their involvement, but this can be far more relaxing than having sleepless nights and frayed nerves!

Not many people fully understand the Planning and Building Control system (*see* Chapter 2). Whilst the local authority is usually very willing to provide assistance, when it can, this can be no more than overall guidance on making applications. However, when matters become complicated and you need to negotiate, you will need specific advice, for example, especially with change of use applications and listed buildings. The Building Regulations can be a minefield for anyone not familiar with them, and difficulties are often encountered when specialist advice has not been obtained. Also, you must be careful not to start work without the necessary approvals, otherwise the local authority can issue you with a 'stop notice' requiring that the works cease immediately. They can also demand that you remove any work not in compliance with the Regulations and require you to reinstate the parts of the building affected.

A major error often made is to fail to check on ground conditions, contamination or on the condition of major structural elements. Without professional advice you may well be storing up problems, which inevitably will cost you dear later on. Structural problems, contamination and ground works can swallow up large amounts of cash without anything tangible to show for it. It is extremely easy to underestimate time and costs. This is one of the major pitfalls, leading to arguments, frustration and tears along the way. If you have never been instrumental in procuring building work, it is better to get professional advice.

The importance of setting a realistic budget cannot be overemphasized. Many people fail to allow sufficient for service connections to isolated buildings, the cost of temporary accommodation whilst the works are in progress and repayments on any loans. Also, most people underestimate the cost of external works such as drives, patios, landscaping and so on. This element can amount to up to 10 per cent of the overall project. It should also be borne in mind that the internal services such as heating, lighting and plumbing can amount to another 30 per cent. But where do you start in setting a realistic budget? Do you ask a recommended local builder, electrician and heating contractor? Does this commit you to using them and can you rely on their estimates? Have you included everything? Have you enough in your budget to allow for the inevitable changes of mind? Do you have a contingency, and if so how much? An architect will be able to assist, especially if he is preparing the plans for you. You should be especially clear regarding the likely costs of changing your mind. You may think that the potential for making changes is included in the original builder's estimate, but you will then have a shock when bills for extras start to appear. We all at some time change our minds, and this has become a recognized and traditional way for builders to realize extra profit after putting in a low initial bid. The real issue is who values the extras. Here again an architect will monitor and advise on the cost of these.

Quality control of the works is essential if you are to avoid problems such as damp penetration, structural inadequacy and lack of heat. You need to ensure also that the finished project can be insured and that any future claims will not be discounted as a result of defects that were present when the conversion works were undertaken. Unless you can inspect the works adequately, it is preferable to use an independent adviser such as an architect or surveyor.

Not paying sufficient attention at the outset and not adequately planning for the installation of internal services usually causes problems later on in the project. Half of the services installation – known as the 'first fix' – takes place at an early stage, for example socket outlet wall boxes and the wiring are installed prior to plastering and heating pipe runs will be installed prior to floors being completed. Once the 'first fix' is finished, it can prove difficult and quite expensive to alter the lighting and heating. It is a good plan to decide how you are going to use the spaces and discuss the services requirement with the architect. It is helpful to plan your furniture layout at this stage and not leave it until the end of the project. You may want some degree of flexibility, and, if so, this should be made clear. The architect will include on his drawings the items that have been agreed; they will be clearly identifiable and can always be taken into account should other things change.

Paying for work too quickly or in advance is a common issue. When the contractor submits his stage payment, how are you to know that the sum is realistic and reflects the work undertaken, or whether or has he charged for work yet to be undertaken or materials yet to be delivered? If you pay too much and in advance any dispute is going to be more difficult to resolve, as the contractor will already have your money and there will be little incentive for him to remedy defects or complete the works. Should a contractor go bankrupt holding money you are trying to reclaim, there is little you can do other than become a creditor. Architects will as a matter of course check stage payments thoroughly and when satisfied that the claim is valid will issue a certificate for payment detailing what retentions are being held. This ensures you only pay for works completed and materials on site; the retention also gives some allowance for you to employ another contractor should the original one default.

Contractual difficulties between contractors and their clients are all too common. Most can be avoided if a formal contract or agreement has been set up prior to the works commencing on site. This should itemize exactly what is going to be done, by whom, by when and for how much. Such agreements are much better prepared by architects or surveyors, who will include specifications and drawings in the document, along with clauses to safeguard your rights as well as those of the contractor. If there is a dispute, a third-party arbitrator or adjudicator can use this document as evidence, making it a lot easier for a fair judgment to be reached.

What Advice Do You Need?

Architects These have the ability to transform your ideas into the built form. An architect will have the necessary design skills to be able to manipulate space effectively while taking into account your requirements versus the constraints of the property chosen.

Structural Engineers A structural engineer may be necessary to advise on the design of supporting structures, such as roofs, floors and so on. You would also need one if, for example, you envisage new or larger openings for windows and doors, or intend major remodelling of the supporting walls.

Quantity Surveyors These may be useful if the anticipated budget is relatively large. A quantity surveyor will provide accurate pre-contract estimates, prepare 'Bills of Quantities' (schedules of the elements that go to make up the project), and provide regular cost reports as the project progresses. He will settle the final account with the contractor.

Solicitors A solicitor is usually required for conveyancing, carrying out local searches and advising on suitable local professionals such as architects. A solicitor is likely to be the first point of contact after the estate agent.

Building Surveyors Use a building surveyor to obtain condition and/or dilapidation surveys on the property chosen.

What Initial Advice is Available?

Architects will normally provide an initial consultation free of charge, especially if the proposals are serious and works are likely to proceed. However, an architect is quite justified in seeking reimbursement for any time spent on the project, especially if the initial meeting is protracted. You may like to consider

'The Architect in the House' scheme run by the Royal Institute of British Architects (RIBA). This is a national event, which allows architects to open their offices to the public and provide consultations free of charge providing a nominal donation is made to charity. Architects will also advise on whether or not other professionals are required and advise on a suitable budget, contractural procedure and programme of works.

The Planning Authority will advise on whether or not a property is suitable for conversion. It will also confirm whether the building is listed or in a conservation area. The local building inspector will advise on specific requirements such as foundations.

The Countryside Agency can give guidance on the conversion of derelict and redundant buildings in the countryside. It publishes various guides on design and planning, some of which are available free of charge.

SPAB (the Society for the Protection of Ancient Buildings) produces various leaflets. These are available from some estate agents and planning offices and deal with the difficulties of converting old buildings and give advice on how to retain the original character and features. The various National Parks and Areas of Outstanding Natural Beauty (AONB) produce guides on the conversion of old buildings, which can be downloaded from the Internet.

ARCHITECTS

Architects can manage all aspects of property conversion and are qualified to project-manage a scheme from inception to completion. Architects are able to look after the intentions and interests of a client. They can produce sketch schemes in sufficient detail to let you appreciate the form and character of any proposal. They can carry out condition and measured surveys. They will analyse the characteristics and constraints of a site or property and will develop a practical, workable and economic solution to fit their clients' aspirations.

They will make all the required applications, on your behalf, to the local authority for planning consent, and also, if necessary, will apply for Listed Building or Conservation Area Consent. They also submit applications, on your behalf, for Building

Regulations Approval and liaise with the local building inspector.

They will prepare working drawings and specifications and also invite suitable contractors to submit competitive tenders. They will advise on timescales and on the appropriate form of contract between you and the main contractor. They will formally instruct the contractor on variations during the contract and will recommend stage payments and agree the final account. They will monitor the progress of the works and ensure that quality is being maintained.

All architects must be registered by ARB (Architects Registration Board), which was set up in 1997 by Act of Parliament to be the independent regulator for the profession and was given a strong mandate to protect the interests of consumers. This latter point is underlined by the fact that out the total board of fifteen, there are eight lay members representing the public interests. ARB is required to maintain an accurate register of those entitled to call themselves 'architect' and has powers to prosecute anyone who uses the title but is not an architect. ARB insists that all registered architects are properly qualified, abide by strict rules of conduct, carry appropriate levels of Professional Indemnity Insurance (PII) and undertake continual professional training. ARB operates an efficient complaints service

and its professional committee will examine any architect's performance and work that may fall short of the expected standards. In the rare case that an architect is found to be negligent, the committee has the powers to reprimand, penalize suspend or remove him or her from the register.

Most architects are also 'Chartered', which means that they are corporate members of the RIBA, or in Scotland the RIAS (Royal Incorporation of Architects in Scotland), and can thus use the suffix RIBA or RIAS after their name. The RIBA monitors the quality of the education given to architects and promotes architecture in the wider sense.

Architects' Fees and Service

Architects normally charge fees as a percentage of the total build cost, usually in the region of 10 per cent for new work. They will normally require a slightly larger percentage for conversion work, which is less straightforward, and extra for extensive interior design work. Some architects will work on a lump-sum basis. It is advisable to establish the basis of charging at the outset, as it often leads to misunderstanding. The RIBA provides guidelines as to recommended fee scales.

Nowadays, the RIBA prefers to allow competition between architects and to let them negotiate with

The architect's fee table should be treated only as a rough and ready reckoner. It will show a fee percentage for any given construction cost. First, take your estimated cost and run this up vertically to the curved line, then go across horizontally to the appropriate fee percentage. For example, for a cost of £100,000 the fee percentage indicated is just over 12 per cent. (© RIBA Enterprises)

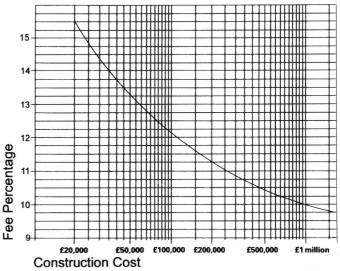

Architect's Fee Guide

individual clients in order to agree a fee appropriate to the services provided and the nature of the project. However, most architects still refer to these scales in their minds when quantifying fees, and it is useful for clients to know, before employing an architect, what they are likely to be charged. It is worth noting that while the fee table indicates an appropriate fee percentage, this may well be discounted upon discussion of your requirements with the architect.

Some work can be done on an hourly rate, especially if the scope of the commission is unclear and/or only partial services are required. However, any fees charged under hourly rates are normally rebated once a full commission is agreed. For guidance, architects normally use the table below to apportion fees to RIBA work stages.

The new *Consultancy Agreement for a home owner/occupier*, published by the Joint Contracts Tribunal (JCT), refers to architects' fees and allows for a total fee, which is split into four stage payments. These stages are detailed in the Agreement and are based on the normal RIBA work stages. The amount of fee required at each stage depends generally on the amount of work the architect is anticipating at each stage.

Explaining what is intended is often difficult. Architects have the necessary skills to turn your thoughts into a project and have the ability to get the work done. Do not be afraid to ask for further explanation if anything is unclear or you feel that your wishes are being sidelined. After all, it is your project and you are paying for the works to be carried out.

However, be prepared to listen to advice; after all, an architect will normally have done this before.

Exactly what the architect is going to undertake for you should be settled at the outset; if not misunderstandings may arise later about who is doing what. Thus the initial meeting is very important and all those who will be involved in using or living in the completed building should be present in order to be aware of what has been agreed and what overall programme is required to achieve completion. Most architects will confirm in writing at the start what services will be provided and how much they will charge.

This 'letter of appointment' helps to establish a proper business footing with the client, who is expected to reply in writing regarding agreement with the scope of the works and programme. Alternatively, the JCT's new *Consultancy Agreement for a home owner/occupier* can be used (*see* Chapter 7 for further information). This sets out the conditions of appointment for the employment of a consultant, is particularly easy to follow, and covers all aspects of the service the consultant will provide, the fees that will be charged, instructing the contractor, issuing certificates and so on.

OPPOSITE: This table shows the various services offered by an architect as categorized by the work stage. The architect and the client need to agree beforehand which stages and services are appropriate for the project.
(© RIBA Enterprises)

Architect Fees at RIBA Work Stages			
Work Stage		**Fee Proportion**	**Cumulative Total**
C	Outline proposals	15%	15%
D	Scheme design	20%	35%
E	Detailed design	20%	55%
F G	Production information and Bills of Quantity	20%	75%
H J K L	Tender action, project planning and operations on site	25%	100%

A–B Inception and Feasibility

01 Obtain information about the Site from the Client
02 Visit the Site and carry out an initial appraisal
03 Assist the Client in preparation of Client's Requirements
04 Advise the Client on methods of procuring construction
05 Advise on the need for specialist contractors, sub-contractors and suppliers to design and execute parts of the Works
06 Prepare proposals and make application for outline planning permission
07 Carry out such studies as may be necessary to determine the feasibility of the Client's Requirements
08 Review with the Client alternative design and construction approaches and cost implications
09 Advise on the need to obtain planning permission, approvals under Building Acts and/or Regulations and other statutory requirements
10 Develop the Client's Requirements
11 Advise on an environmental impact and prepare report
12 ...

C Outline Proposals

01 Analyse the Client's Requirements: prepare outline proposals
02 Provide information to, discuss proposals with and incorporate input of other consultants
03 Provide information to other consultants for their preparation of an approximation of construction cost
03A Prepare an approximation of construction cost
04 Submit outline proposals and approximation of construction cost for the Client's preliminary approval
05 Propose a procedure for cost planning and control
06 Provide information to others for cost planning and control throughout the Project
06A Operate the procedure for cost planning and control throughout the Project
07 Prepare and keep updated a Client's running expenditure plan for the Project
08 Prepare special presentation drawings, brochures, models or technical information for use of the Client or others
09 Carry out negotiations with tenants or others identified by the Client
10 ...

D Scheme Design

01 Develop scheme design from approved outline proposals
02 Provide information to, discuss proposals with and incorporate input of other consultants into scheme design
03 Provide information to other consultants for their preparation of cost estimate
03A Prepare cost estimate
04 Prepare preliminary timetable for construction
05 Consult with planning authorities
06 Consult with building control authorities
07 Consult with fire authorities
08 Consult with environmental authorities
09 Consult with licensing authorities
10 Consult with statutory undertakers
11 Prepare an application for full planning permission
12 Submit scheme design showing spatial arrangements, materials and appearance, together with cost estimate, for the Client's approval
13 Consult with tenants or others identified by the Client
14 Conduct exceptional negotiations with planning authorities
15 Submit an application for full planning permission
16 Prepare multiple applications for full planning permission
17 Submit multiple applications for full planning permission
18 Make revisions to scheme design to deal with requirements of planning authorities
19 Revise planning application
20 Resubmit planning application
21 Carry out special constructional research for the Project including design of prototypes, mock-ups or models
22 Monitor testing of prototypes, mock-ups or models etc.
23 ...

E Detail Design

01 Develop detail design from approved scheme design
02 Provide information to, discuss proposals with and incorporate input of other consultants into detail design
03 Provide information to other consultants for their revision of cost estimate
03A Revise cost estimate
04 Prepare applications for approvals under Building Acts and/or Regulations and other statutory requirements
04A Prepare building notice under Building Acts and/or Regulations*
05 Agree form of building contract and explain the Client's obligations thereunder
06 Obtain the Client's approval of the type of construction, quality of materials and standard of workmanship
07 Apply for approvals under Building Acts and/or Regulations and other statutory requirements
07A Give building notice under Building Acts and/or Regulations*
08 Negotiate if necessary over Building Acts and/or Regulations and other statutory requirements and revise production information
09 Conduct exceptional negotiations for approvals by statutory authorities
10 Negotiate waivers or relaxations under Building Acts and/or Regulations and other statutory requirements
11 ...

F–G Production Information and Bills of Quantities

01 Prepare production drawings
02 Prepare specification
03 Provide information for the preparation of bills of quantities and/or schedules of works
03A Prepare schedule of rates and/or quantities and/or schedules of works for tendering purposes
04 Provide information to, discuss proposals with and incorporate input of other consultants into production information
05 Co-ordinate production information
06 Provide information to other consultants for their revision of cost estimate
06A Revise cost estimate
07 Review timetable for construction
08 Prepare other production information
09 Submit plans for proposed building works for approval of landlords, funders, free-holders, tenants or others as requested by the Client
10 ...

H Tender Action

01 Advise on and obtain the Client's approval to a list of tenderers for the building contract
02 Invite tenders
03 Appraise and report on tenders with other consultants
03A Appraise and report on tenders
04 Assist other consultants in negotiating with a tenderer
04A Negotiate with a tenderer
05 Assist other consultants in negotiating a price with a contractor
05A Negotiate a price with a contractor
06 Select a contractor by other means
07 Revise production information to adjust tender sum
08 Arrange for other contracts to be let prior to the main building contract
09 ...

J Project Planning

01 Advise the Client on the appointment of the contractor and on the responsibilities of the parties and the Architect under the building contract
02 Prepare the building contract and arrange for it to be signed
03 Provide production information as required by the building contract
04 Provide services in connection with demolitions
05 Arrange for other contracts to be let subsequent to the commencement of the building contract
06 ...

19 Incorporate information prepared by others in maintenance manuals
20 Prepare a programme for the maintenance of a building
21 Arrange maintenance contracts
22 ...

K–L Operations on Site and Completion

01 Administer the terms of the building contract
02 Conduct meetings with the contractor to review progress
03 Provide information to other consultants for the preparation of financial reports to the Client
03A Prepare financial reports for the Client
04 Generally inspect materials delivered to the site
05 As appropriate instruct sample taking and carrying out tests of materials, components, techniques and workmanship and examine the conduct and results of such tests whether on or off site
06 As appropriate instruct the opening up of completed work to determine that it is generally in accordance with the Contract Documents
07 As appropriate visit the sites of the extraction and fabrication and assembly of materials and components to inspect such materials and workmanship before delivery to site
08 At intervals appropriate to the stage of construction visit the Works to inspect the progress and quality of the Works and to determine that they are being executed generally in accordance with the Contract Documents
09 Direct and control the activities of Site Staff
10 Provide drawings showing the building and the main lines of drainage
11 Arrange for drawings of building services installations to be provided
12 Give general advice on maintenance
13 Administer the terms of other contracts
14 Monitor the progress of the Works against the contractor's programme and report to the Client
15 Prepare valuations of work carried out and completed
16 Provide specially prepared drawings of a building as built
17 Prepare drawings for conveyancing purposes
18 Compile maintenance and operational manuals

Work Stages are specified by circling the stage letters.

Basic Services indicated by the coloured area are are specified unless struck out.

Additional Services are specified by circling the relevant numbered items.

* Not applicable in Scotland

The RIBA publishes useful guides on the services available from architects, the normal work stages for a project and the percentage of the overall fee required at each stage.

STRUCTURAL ENGINEERS

Structural engineers ensure that everything in a building can support itself and any imposed load. They also ensure that all loads are transmitted safely to adequate foundations. It is advisable to employ a structural engineer when there are works required to existing roof timbers or large structural openings are envisaged.

Structural engineers have to comply with the Building Regulations (Part A – Structure) and the various codes of practice and British Standards. They will be able to survey existing structures and report on what structural repairs and/or modifications are necessary. Along with the architect, a structural engineer will prepare drawings and calculations for the works proposed and obtain the necessary permissions under the Building Regulations. Structural engineers are members of the Institution of Structural Engineers (IstructE) and often ACE (Association of Consulting Engineers). ACE sets the conditions of appointment of all consulting engineers including building services engineers (*see below*). They produce a code of conduct and recommended fee scales. Ensure that the engineer carries PII (Professional Indemnity Insurance) to a value appropriate to the project. Engineers can either charge at an hourly rate (which is preferable) or a percentage of the structural works involved. Normally for small projects this could be 15 per cent. They can also charge a lump sum if the works are not too complex.

Architects can normally recommend a good engineer and will usually know one who is used to working on older properties. You can also find an engineer by logging onto the structural engineers' or the ACE website. It is a good idea to employ a local engineer, who should certainly have knowledge of the local soil conditions and anything peculiar to your area. Use of local consultants also cuts down on travelling time.

QUANTITY SURVEYORS

For very complex schemes and schemes with large budgets it may well be advisable to use the services of a quantity surveyor. A general rule of thumb would be to use a quantity surveyor on projects costing in excess of £150,000.

Quantity surveyors, as their title suggests, deal with the 'quantities' of the materials that make up a building and carry out measurements from the architect's drawing to determine such things as the number of bricks required, areas of paving, cubes of topsoil and so on. These are combined with hourly rates to determine the cost of each element. They provide pre-contract estimates, which can be useful for budgeting and obtaining finance.

They produce 'Bills of Quantities' (B of Qs), which are basically schedules of the elements that

---

Finding an Architect

It is always worth considering a local architect, as he or she will have the advantage of local knowledge and will certainly have experience of the local Planning Authority and suitable contractors. Consider choosing architects who have carried out similar commissions successfully. Ask to visit reference sites and for permission to talk to their clients.

Check an architect's membership of the professional bodies and do not be shy about asking what level of PII (Professional Indemnity Insurance) is held. The minimum these days is £250,000 for smaller practices and sole practitioners, rising to £1,000,000 for medium-sized practices. These figures are monitored by ARB, and are likely to rise in line with any increase in the level of claims experienced and the amount of protection thought necessary to protect the general public.

The RIBA has set up a Clients' Advisory Service (CAS) to assist in the choosing of an architect who is suitable for the type of work envisaged. A register of local architects who can be contacted through the RIBA website is maintained. However, choosing architect who is right for you is not always easy and you could easily be put off before you start. A good way is to seek recommendation, perhaps from local builders and maybe from planners who have worked successfully with local architects.

---

make up a building, for example the quantities of brickwork and timber, the number of doors, the volumes of concrete and so on. The Bill also describes the work involved and the contract programme, and sets out strict requirements for workmanship relating to the Codes of Practice and British Standards. The Bill is used along with the architect's drawings to obtain competitive tenders from contractors. When a Bill is used on a project, there is little room for doubt as to what is intended and the successful contractor is duty bound to provide what is contained in the Bill at an agreed cost, by an agreed date and to an agreed quality.

Quantity surveyors produce pre-tender estimates and recommendations regarding appointing contractors after tender. They value the works as they progress, including any changes, and they make recommendations on stage payments and the final account. They ensure that the client gets value for money. Quantity surveyors are members of the RICS (Royal Institution of Chartered Surveyors), which, like architects, means that they have to abide by strict rules of conduct, carry appropriate levels of professional insurance and undertake continual professional training. Fees are charged in accordance with recommended scales published by the RICS. For most normal work, the fee is not likely to exceed 5 per cent of the cost of the works above a value of £150,000.

The architect would be able to recommend a quantity surveyor suitable for the project; otherwise, contact the RICS website.

LANDSCAPE ARCHITECTS

Landscape architects can provide a very valuable additional service, especially where a site is derelict and largely overgrown. They are helpful if you want to achieve a quick 'finished' result; their work will enhance a building's setting and frequently increases the value of the finished project. They are able to provide a coordinated scheme in both hard and soft landscape and have the ability visualize what is relevant for the site and soil, as well as specifying planting and future maintenance.

A qualified landscape architect will be a chartered member of the Landscape Institute, which specifies

strict codes of conduct. He or she must also carry appropriate levels of professional insurance. You can find a suitable landscape architect by logging onto the Institute's website.

BUILDING SERVICES ENGINEERS

Building services is frequently the area that causes the most problems; the simplest mistakes made at the start of a project can be difficult and costly to remedy later on. It is not commonly realized that building services can be as much as 30 per cent of the budget and therefore deserve to be given careful consideration. It is often the practice to use the 'design and install' capabilities of building services contractors. These can vary a great deal and you should certainly seek recommendation and visit reference sites if possible. The other alternative is to employ a chartered building services engineer, who will be able to provide professional and impartial advice on the various heating, ventilation and electrical systems that are available and suitable for the project. He will produce drawings and specifications for pricing and will supervise the works. He will control the quality and technical standard of the works and agree stage payments to the contractor.

Planning building service installations carefully and thoroughly will reap benefits, and by using a building services engineer you may be saved a lot of trouble and money in the end. Whilst they are normally employed on commercial schemes, one should certainly consider employing an engineer where unconventional or technically advanced installations are envisaged. You should also consider one especially if you are considering high-energy efficiency schemes.

Chartered building service engineers are normally members of CIBSE (the Chartered Institution of Building Service Engineers) and a suitable engineer can be found be using their website.

OTHERS

Building Surveyors

A building surveyor can advise on repairs and demolitions and can be the best choice if you are considering large amounts of remedial works, with only a small amount of remodelling. Unlike architects, the title 'surveyor' is not protected, hence anyone can call themselves a surveyor.

You should therefore only use chartered surveyors, that is, those who are members of the RICS (Royal Institution of Chartered Surveyors). They will carry appropriate PII and will be required to adhere to strict codes of conduct.

Planning Consultants

Planning consultants have arisen to cope with the complexities and vagaries of the Town and Country Planning Acts. This profession focuses primarily on the highly specialized area of planning applications and dealing with planning appeals. Normally, it is the architect who deals with planning applications, but if difficulties are envisaged the architect may advise that a planning consultant be employed.

Planning consultants are generally qualified town planners or occasionally solicitors. Many will have worked for local authorities prior to practising on their own account. They are most useful when dealing with difficult and complex planning situations, especially when a proposal is in conflict with the Local Development Plan for the area.

Planning Supervisors

This is a new class of consultant (not to be confused with Planning Consultants) who have appeared as a result of the Construction (Design and Management) Regulations 1994, known as the CDM Regulations (*see* Chapter 2). The Regulations *do not* normally apply to domestic property but the architect (or designer), however, has a duty to comply with them even so and his design will need to take into account aspects of health and safety. He will also deal with the HSE (Health & Safety Executive) notification on your behalf.

Should planning supervision be required it is normally an additional service provided by building and quantity surveyors, architects or engineers.

Building Technicians

These may be members of the BIAT (British Institute of Architectural Technologists) and architects normally employ them in their offices as CAD (computer-aided design) technicians or draughtsmen. Some may have broadened their experience and skills sufficiently to be able to design and specify, and also to manage building projects very effectively.

You should avoid any 'technician' who is not a member of BIAT, as there is no guarantee of competence or experience. Lots of people associated with the building industry call themselves technicians or surveyors without the proper qualifications and they are unlikely to carry indemnity insurance. Some are also known as 'plan drawers'. It is often the case that an unqualified 'technician', 'surveyor' or 'plan drawer' is much cheaper to employ, but their service in no way compares to that of the properly qualified individual. There is little redress against such an unqualified person if things go wrong.

Useful Information and Contacts

- Royal Institute of British Architects: Tel. 020 7307 3700; *www.architecture.com*
- Royal Incorporation of Architects in Scotland (RIAS): Tel. 0131 229 7545; *www.rias.org.uk*
- Royal Society of Ulster Architects (RSUA): Tel. 0289 0323 760; *www.rsua.org.uk*
- Royal Institute of the Architects of Ireland (RIAI): Tel. +353(0) 1 676 1703; *www.riai.ie*
- Architects Registration Board (ARB): Tel. 020 7580 5861; *www.arb.org.uk*
- Royal Institution of Chartered Surveyors (RICS): Tel. 0870 333 1600; *www.rics.org.uk*
- Institute of Structural Engineers: *www.instructe.org.uk*
- Association of Consulting Engineers (ACE): Tel. 020 7222 6557; *www.acenet.co.uk*
- Chartered Institution of Building Services Engineers (CIBSE): Tel. 020 8675 5211; *www.cibse.org.uk*
- The Landscape Institute: Tel. 020 7350 5200; *www.l-a.org.uk*
- British Institute of Architectural Technologists (BIAT): Tel. 020 7278 2206; *www.biat.org.uk*
- Society for the Protection of Ancient Buildings (SPAB): Tel. 020 7377 1644; *www.spab.org.uk*
- Countryside Agency: Tel. 020 7340 2900; *www.countryside.gov.uk*

CHAPTER 5

The Design Brief

INCEPTION

Before embarking on any construction project, it is essential to know what it is you want to achieve. In order to be clear in one's own mind or to instruct anyone else who may become involved in the project, a design brief will need to be prepared. A precise and clear brief is fundamental to the overall success and smooth process in achieving your goal.

Careful analysis of exactly what you and your family want is strongly advised well before you approach any professionals, otherwise much time and money can be wasted if there are conflicts. Nothing is more frustrating than a couple who have not considered carefully what they want to achieve together before a meeting with a professional, who then disagree on many fundamental issues in front of him or her!

What is a Design Brief? and What Should it Contain?

You should sit down and consider your requirements under various headings (as suggested in the Briefing Questionnaire below). Your answers to these questions will enable you to test any design solutions. It is very important for you to put sufficient time aside at this stage, although it is not appropriate to get too involved in planning layouts or designing, otherwise you will become bogged down in the detail with too many conflicts and ideas. However, it is good practice to record any initial thoughts and sketches for future reference. These can be dealt with later, during the detailed design phase. The design brief stage is a simple process of trying to focus on *what* activities the building will need to accommodate, not *how*. It should be inception rather than feasibility.

In the case of conversions, you need to be aware that the building chosen may not be able to accommodate all the desired activities and space requirements. Therefore, you need to list your priorities and be prepared to compromise. If there is still a problem, you may have to go elsewhere! By carrying out this initial analysis, you will have probably saved on time and professional fees if things do not look like working out. However, there is a 'Catch 22' situation, in that to be able to prove that the activities can or cannot be accommodated, you will probably need the services of an architect or designer. He can use his design skills and knowledge of the basic room sizes and shapes to make the most of the space available, and should be able to produce a workable design solution to meet most situations.

Briefing Questionnaire

A design brief is built up of answers to a series of questions, such as: Do you like open plan or a more traditional cellular configuration of rooms? Do you like changes in level? Would you consider having your living rooms above your bedrooms? Do you want the kitchen at the heart of the house? Do you need a study or playroom, and where should they be in relation to the main living rooms? Do you have hobbies or interests that would influence the design, for instance a piano or entertainment centre that would have to be accommodated or designed around? Do you put your car in a garage? Do you have a boat that requires storage, or need a drying room for outdoor clothes or wet suits?

The Briefing Questionnaire suggests typical questions under various headings and it is the answers to these that will have a bearing on the final solution. You should set aside sufficient time and write down your answers with any additional comments (you can modify them later). You and your family should participate in the session to avoid future conflicts!

	Briefing Questionnaire	
Category	**Question**	**Answer/Comment**
1. Lifestyle	• Do you want seclusion or to be part of a community? • Do you want a garden? Small or large? Ease of maintenance? Hard and/or soft landscaping? Courtyard? • Do you have an outdoor lifestyle or activities? Do you want a barbeque area? • Do you entertain? Capacity of dining room? • Do members of the family have any conflicting lifestyles? Hi-fi? Television? Homework? Musical instrument? Office? • Do you collect things?	
2. Bedrooms	• Present requirements? • Future requirements? • En-suite requirements?	
3. Accommodation for guests	• Do you require any extra bedrooms with or without en-suite facilities?	
4. Extended family	• Are your parents to live with you? • Are grown up children living with you?	
5. Storage	• Do you require closets? Fitted wardrobes? Built-in cupboards? • Do you want loft storage? • Do you require external storage or sheds? • Will you require fuel storage? Coal? Oil? LPG? Logs? • Do you want to store wine?	
6. Work rooms/home office	• Do you have hobbies that have particular space requirements? • Do you work from home and have particular requirements? • Do you require any workshop facilities?	
7. Utility spaces	• Do you want a specific laundry area? • Do you require any areas for washing down and cleaning? • Where do you want to site your freezers?	

Category	Question	Answer/Comment
8. Play areas	• Do require a playroom? Nursery? • Any provision to be made for an external play area?	
9. Pets and animals	• Are there any specific internal arrangements? • Are there any specific external requirements? Kennel? Stables? Hutches?	
10. Bathrooms and shower rooms	• Number of full bathrooms required? Shower rooms? • Do you require any to be en-suite? • Cloakroom facility?	
11. Relationship between rooms and exterior	• What relationship is required between kitchen, dining and living spaces? • What relationship is required between interior and external spaces? • Where will you enter the building? • Are there front and back doors? • What does the hallway lead into and how is it approached from where the car is parked?	
12. Facilities for motor cars, motorcycles and bicycles	• Do you require a garage? Number of vehicles to be accommodated? • Do you want a carport? • Do you require parking? • Are you intending to carry out vehicle maintenance?	
13. Heating and energy conservation	• Are there any 'Green' issues that you would like to pursue? • What type of fuel do you propose using? • Have you a preferred heating system? • Do you require an open fire or wood-burning stove?	
14. Expansion and flexibility	• Do you require any space to be flexible, such as study/bedroom? • Do you need the ability to extend? • Would you require a conservatory?	
15. Views	• Does the kitchen need to overlook the access drive, the garden, face north or the view? • Are there views to be maintained?	
16. Privacy and security	• Do you have issues with noise? Neighbours? • Do you want total privacy? • Do you want good security?	

FEASIBILITY

Having formalized your requirements it is time to examine the site and building in more detail, so as to arrive at the best design to fit your needs. It is at this stage that professionals should be employed. If you have prepared the design brief adequately, then any architect approached is very likely to be impressed by your preparedness and knowledge, and, consequently, the work should proceed much more smoothly.

Constraints and Opportunities

As with all building projects, site analysis is the essential launching point for the successful integration of conversion work into the existing structure. The added challenge of conversions is the number of constraints that the designer is confronted with at the outset, such as structural walls in the wrong place, windows and doors that are restricted in location or tie beams at chest level should a new upper floor be introduced. The skill of the designer is to utilize these features by working round them and including those you wish to retain. It may require the ground floor to be lowered or the roof structure to be altered, but whatever the problems the overall appeal of the initial building – be it school, chapel, warehouse or barn – must not be lost by insensitive additions or alterations inside or out.

Aspect and orientation have to be considered early on for the successful planning of the main living areas. Your lifestyle, as outlined in the design brief, will be taken into account at the same time as deciding what goes where. In courtyard groups shared external circulation is sometimes necessary in the court or farmyard and can provide parking and access to the dwellings. This can allow the outward-facing walls to be punctuated with openings onto private areas of garden.

In chapels the problems of symmetry as well as height have to be considered without loss of dignified space. Galleries and aisles have to be made into the

OPPOSITE: The translucent glazed screen allows light to filter into the windowless hallway. (Nigel Rigden)

Entrance to courtyard through an old cart access. Note the door to the hayloft. (Barrie Davies)

domestic offices, probably leaving the nave as the grand circulation and formal living space. This approach could help also to avoid costly heating bills if the central area is treated as a covered external space or atrium.

In warehouse conversions, there can be a great depth of floor plan but limited external wall space. Here, service cores can help to reduce the width of living areas by being positioned next to external walls. Double-height or two-storey conversions in these circumstances can offer more dramatic effects, with sections of floor removed, so as to allow natural light to penetrate much further into the building.

Borrowed lights to deep internal spaces can look institutional if not considered properly; they need to be carefully integrated into the design of the wall into which they are to be inserted. Opaque full-height glazed screens may well be appropriate with the right interior design scheme in these situations.

Column grids can also help to define zones without obstructing the free flow of space that is the most attractive feature of many industrial conversions.

The introduction of intermediate or mezzanine floors into large-volume formal spaces such as schools

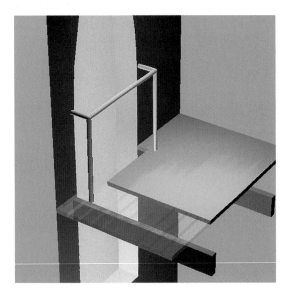

The floor structure is set back from the window, allowing the external elevation of the window to be uninterrupted. (Barrie Davies)

and chapels can be a most difficult alteration to achieve successfully. Some early conversions clearly expressed the depth of the introduced floor where it collided with the external windows, often destroying the sense of proportion or even the windows' characteristics. Ways can be found of avoiding this situation by careful design, such as stopping the new floor short of the wall but allowing the joists to carry on to the supporting wall. Daylight can then filter through the exposed joists whilst keeping the tall windows intact.

ARCHITECTURAL STYLE

The very nature of a conversion project is the reuse of an existing building worthy of conversion and that building will have a character of its own. This character should be respected and help to determine ideas to be incorporated into the design of the project.

In barns and chapels, very strong structural and architectural features may abound. All planning authorities are aware of this and planning policy guidelines consequently attain to the sensitivity of conversion work on the existing vernacular and historic building stock. However, it is not necessary or even appropriate in most cases slavishly to copy an existing detail or feature. Besides probably being prohibitively expensive, it is the role of the designer to echo the character of the building by reinterpretation. It is also the aim of most conservation officers these days to encourage this approach to conversion.

Elements that are to be retained will have been normally identified at the key measured survey stage of the project (*see* Chapter 1). Details of the structural features of walls and roofs, particularly timberwork, should be measured, along with windows, doors and any mouldings around openings. The layout of bays and structural partitions should also be measured, as this will be fundamental in achieving a successful and sympathetic layout.

The reinstatement of features that have decayed or been lost by past negligence or insensitive repair is often encouraged, for example the replacement of roof truss members in native hardwood using traditional jointing methods. It will then be desirable for these features to be incorporated into the design of the conversion and this will suggest the disposition of

A gallery constructed to echo the structure of the existing roof. (Nigel Rigden)

the new accommodation. The approach has to be much more 'fitting into the existing' than moulding the existing to suit a preconceived set of requirements. That is why it is so important to discuss the compatibility of one's ideas with the area planning office before purchasing a building for conversion and being aware of the policies and guidelines that are adhered to locally. It is the history of incompetent and insensitive conversions that has led to the enforcement of strict guidelines now – although the interpretation of what is appropriate varies widely from one district council to another. Each case has to be assessed individually, as the site can be as important an issue as the actual building that is to be converted. Most councils, however, prefer to see as little interruption to the existing external envelope as possible. Style, therefore, is not usually an option, but rather the method of retaining the existing character.

In buildings of 'lesser quality', in planning parlance, that are still worthy of retention and conversion, there is more scope for reinterpretation. In these cases, contemporary elements, such as mezzanine floors, galleries and open-tread stairways with plain balustrading, can be introduced to enhance the intrinsic qualities of the existing building.

Sometimes a new independent structural timber or steel frame can be introduced to support the new elements, whilst strengthening and bracing the existing structures.

Steel beams and columns installed to form a new mezzanine floor and to support new door openings. (Nigel Rigden)

Internal finishes are also crucial in retaining character, and Building Regulations requirements in relation to insulation are making it increasingly difficult to leave large areas of masonry or timber boarding exposed. Insulated plasterboard dry lining is now common on the inside of external walls as it can cover old blemishes, unevenness and even holes, whilst making living in a large void thermally bearable and relatively economic. Waviness and outward-leaning walls can still be expressed, but behind a new plastered surface. Rougher finishes can also look appropriate with the right mix artfully applied. These can also now be supplied coloured in a range of earthy hues, which can contribute to the 'warmth' of the building. Exposed roof timbers and large beams also differentiate barns from normal residential accommodation.

Old oak and elm timbers can provide much interest and will retain the agricultural character of a building if treated sympathetically and will add maturity to the conversion. Where areas of masonry or brickwork are of sufficient quality to be left exposed, the correct pointing mix and texture are essential to complement the walling. This can also add warmth to the otherwise potentially cold surface of an agricultural building.

The external colours of woodwork finishes are also matters of concern to many councils, and are sometimes included as conditions attached to planning approval documents, with English hardwoods often stipulated. These woods, for example oak and chestnut, can weather to a silvery grey or soft honey colour that complements and harmonizes with the masonry or weather boarding of the original walling.

The roof timbers and oak posts dominate this living space. (Nigel Rigden)

The oak used in the panelling and doors to this barn has weathered to a silver-grey colour. The original brown colour can be seen on the top of the doorway to the right of the picture. (Nigel Rigden)

An existing orchard has been allowed to form part of the garden and has been enhanced by planting new apple trees. (Nigel Rigden)

BELOW: Oak posts have been retained and new ones added to help form room dividers. (Nigel Rigden)

The interior frame of this former oast house dominates this mezzanine bedroom space.
(Nigel Rigden)

Stains applied to timber should be black or dark brown in colour in order for barns to retain their robust weathered appearance. In chapels, mills and industrial conversions white or even black paint may be appropriate for cast-iron windows or replacements that echo the original.

Externally, minimum interference to the original setting is often stipulated, with the common domestic landscaping features such as conservatories and pergolas discouraged. Full landscaping proposals are normally required at the planning stage. These will need to be considered as a whole, and take into account the building in its context with such items as boundary treatment and parking surfaces. Planting should reflect the indigenous species associated with the region in which the project is located. Native trees and shrubs for hedging and replanting orchards can help in retaining the traditional farmyard appearance of the original.

Space Planning

The division of space is amongst the most difficult of alterations to achieve successfully in conversion work. If the large volume of space provided by the original shell is poorly subdivided, and the original architectural interest removed or hidden, then the reason for choosing the building for conversion in

the first place will have been lost. Respect for the soul of the building is paramount in retaining the character and unique appeal of the conversion project.

It is not usually possible when creating a home from a barn or chapel to leave the whole structure open and uninterrupted. The need for the partition and division of space to create the various rooms required for residential use has to be very carefully considered at an early stage. It is sometimes not possible to balance the needs of the prospective purchaser with the existing building and the requirements of the planners. The planners seldom agree to wholesale removal or remodelling of historically valuable structures. So if compromise is not possible it would be better to look elsewhere. The various district councils interpret the current Department of the Environment requirements differently and Areas of Outstanding Natural Beauty (AONBs) or National Parks can be particularly difficult areas in which to negotiate relaxations of the regulations.

Sometimes the interior structural frame is also part of the listing and these dominant features have to be integrated into quite small domestic spaces such as bedrooms and bathrooms. While they can add much character to the project, they can also be made to look out of place by ill-considered planning that fails to take account of the geometry, form and bulk of the structure.

As well as strong structural grids or bays, many conversions have to be accommodated within linear plan forms such as former cow stalls. These are often completely open on one side with blank walls on the other. How does one avoid long, dark corridors and the railway carriage effect? A possible solution is to group the living rooms centrally, with bedrooms at either end. However, while this is an ideal arrangement when guests visit, it is not particularly appropriate for families with young children, whose bedrooms may need to be within easy reach of their parents'. If the building width and roof pitch allow, mezzanine gallery spaces can be formed in the roof voids over the bedrooms, leaving the roof void open over the living area to reveal the structure and character of the original building. Flush-fitting roof lights can often be utilized as windows in this situation so that the line of the roof is not broken.

The structure and character of the roof of this former barn have been retained and enhanced to provide the main theme of this interior. (Nigel Rigden)

Corridors are to be avoided as far as possible as they are costly and use much valuable space, although sometimes they cannot be avoided to make linear plans work. In these circumstances they can become an event, perhaps top-lit if new openings in walls are restricted and used as display areas for paintings.

In addition, by creating bays at doorways to interrupt the length and by omitting ceilings the roof can become a dramatic intervention, revealing elements of structure not seen elsewhere in the building.

EXTERNAL OPENINGS AND NATURAL LIGHT

The provision of natural light can present problems with existing buildings that have relatively few openings. For instance, some barns have blank walls to the roadside elevation and planning officers often like to see these retained with no new openings permitted. However, the other flank walls will probably have a variety of openings, ranging from two-storey double doors to narrow ventilation slits with splayed reveals.

This corridor with its low ceiling and single high-level window has provided an opportunity to display a wall hanging effectively. (Nigel Rigden)

The ventilation slot of this former listed tithe barn has been retained and glazed. (Barrie Davies)

It may also be possible to open a section of roof and replace it with an area of glazing that follows the line of the roof and brings much light into the heart of the building. Planning officers are more likely to accept a bold intervention that relates well to the form and scale of the building than the insertion of standard cottage-style timber casement windows of a domestic scale. Doors and windows, as the eyes of the building, have to be well thought-out to achieve or maintain balance, character and rhythm. The successful division of large areas of glazing is also important to echo the character of the building. Use of standard joinery rarely looks appropriate in conversion work as the building to be converted is not originally of a domestic scale.

The small openings that bathrooms and WCs require for windows mean that they can often be housed in the roof, utilizing rooflights, which retain roof form, are more economical to install and are less obtrusive than dormers. Bathrooms also benefit from the use of lay lights, as they afford privacy without the need for opaque glazing, while also leaving uninterrupted wall surfaces for mirrors, tiling, shelves and ductwork. This approach also allows the living rooms, which need good natural light, to benefit from the existing openings. These openings can often be very large, but can also be at a premium if planning restrictions limit the installation of new openings in order to retain the character of the original building.

OPPOSITE: The roof glazing of this dining space has become the main focal point of the room. It is also positioned directly over the glazed floor, to provide light to the entrance lobby below. (Nigel Rigden)

The inserted roof glazing echoes the colour and scale of the adjoining slate roofs and allows the opportunity for top lighting the stairwells. (Nigel Rigden)

The roof structure of this barn has been retained, but has been floored over in part to provide a gallery overlooking the main living space.
(Nigel Rigden)

The position of existing openings can also lead to safety difficulties that have to be considered under the Building Regulations legislation. Low or even floor level sill heights are common and will require careful detailing to accommodate safety glass and protective railings as unobtrusively and appropriately as possible. Existing openings may also only be located on the worst side of the building (the north side), or may overlook a neighbouring property or a high wall that cannot be removed. Here, bold interventions such as light wells or roof glazing may have to be considered, or perhaps internal courts that are overlooked by internal galleries.

Innovation may be required and it takes an experienced and skilled hand to achieve natural illumination successfully if only a limited light source is available.

PRIVACY AND ACOUSTICS

The current trend for large living areas into which the kitchen, breakfast or dining room and family sitting room are all combined has had a major influence on building size and room layout. The barn or chapel conversion is in many ways an ideal vehicle for this fashion, as the space required for such a large hub to the home is often available in abundance in the larger volumes offered by older institutional buildings. In a barn or chapel the height available can give this central core an even more dramatic presence in the building. The roof structure may be of sufficient merit to leave it open from the ground and perhaps a section of the first floor or ceiling could be left out to give the opportunity for galleries or a robustly detailed timber stairway rising out of the living area.

Off this core can radiate the quieter zones of bedrooms and work and study areas, possibly separated by tall structural walls that are also acoustically efficient.

Open-plan living is difficult to reconcile with good acoustic separation – the noise of teacups can be very penetrating, especially if the kitchen is linked to the remainder of the house by doorless corridors. Acoustic separation therefore needs to be carefully considered early on in the design stage, as it is notoriously difficult to achieve and very expensive when done in retrospect. However, by careful planning and use of the heavy elements of the existing structure, the noisy and quiet areas can be successfully separated in a passive way.

MATERIALS

The shell of the original structure can often be the subject of planning restrictions or conditions in the council's approval for conversion. Existing materials and their appearance in terms of weathering and maturing have to be carefully considered and treated with respect. The right approach has to be sought in repairing or adding to these structures, so that the alterations are unobtrusive or any extension is appropriate in scale, detailing and use of materials.

Natural stone or old brick walls often need re-pointing or require new openings to be formed

The new garage and outbuildings faithfully reflect the form and structure of the main building and are in harmony as to colour and texture. (Nigel Rigden)

A quiet sitting area has been provided on a landing, well away from the main living areas. (Nigel Rigden)

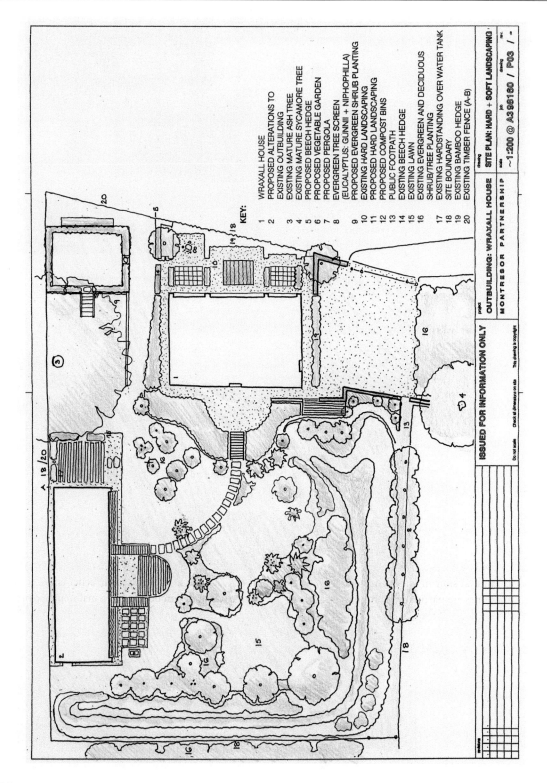

KEY:

1   WRAXALL HOUSE
2   PROPOSED ALTERATIONS TO
    EXISTING OUTBUILDING
3   EXISTING MATURE ASH TREE
4   EXISTING MATURE SYCAMORE TREE
5   PROPOSED BEECH HEDGE
6   PROPOSED VEGETABLE GARDEN
7   PROPOSED PERGOLA
8   EVERGREEN TREE SCREEN
    (EUCALYPTUS: GUNNII + NIPHOPHILLA)
9   PROPOSED EVERGREEN SHRUB PLANTING
10 EXISTING HARD LANDSCAPING
11 PROPOSED HARD LANDSCAPING
12 PROPOSED COMPOST BINS
13 PUBLIC FOOTPATH
14 EXISTING BEECH HEDGE
15 EXISTING LAWN
16 EXISTING EVERGREEN AND DECIDUOUS
    SHRUB/TREE PLANTING
17 EXISTING HARDSTANDING OVER WATER TANK
18 SITE BOUNDARY
19 EXISTING BAMBOO HEDGE
20 EXISTING TIMBER FENCE (A-B)

ISSUED FOR INFORMATION ONLY

Do not scale   Check all dimensions on site   This drawing is copyright

| project | OUTBUILDING: WRAXALL HOUSE |
| MONTRESOR PARTNERSHIP | |

| drawing | SITE PLAN: HARD + SOFT LANDSCAPING |
| scale ~1:200 @ A3 | job A3 96160 | drawing / P03 | rev. / - |

92

The boldness, colour and texture of the gravel drive are complementary to the form and colours of the converted barn. (Nigel Rigden)

during the conversion process. Local advice is strongly recommended regarding the use of the right mortar for the facing material and its aspect in terms of weathering. Mortar colour is very important, as is the method of jointing, but the content of the mix is the most crucial aspect. The wrong mix can radically affect the balance of the wall, its long-term weather resistance and erosion of the facing material. Some softer limestones are particularly prone to weathering and frost damage if mortar with cement content is applied. Local listed building officers often provide pamphlets on the correct mixes and profiles for the area.

OPPOSITE: A typical drawing detailing landscaping proposals. The drawing indicates both hard and soft landscaping along with any existing tress and shrubs to be retained. (Montresor Partnership)

It is sometimes difficult to match exactly old stone and brickwork, as many quarries and small brickworks have long since closed. Usually a close match is available from elsewhere, such as reclamation yards, but local knowledge is essential to be sure of ordering the right type and sizes of stone to be compatible with the existing materials. Lime renders are now also more readily available and their benefits are understood so that design details and a maintenance procedure can be adopted.

An alternative approach to matching and blending is to form a break in style and material where significant alterations or an extension are to abut the existing structure. This is not easy to carry off with conviction and it is not for the faint-hearted, as it may well require additional prolonged negotiations with the planning authorities. It is important that the choice of professional matches your aesthetic aspirations if this course is to be chosen.

93

EXTERNAL DESIGN

The setting of the existing building is often going to be at odds with the eventual result of the conversion project. Farmyards and graveyards are far removed from most people's traditional vision of a garden. City conversions likewise will probably be short of amenable external areas, as factories and offices are more likely to share public courts, car parks or service yards than to enjoy private gardens.

The combination of appropriate landscaping and plants with well-chosen materials for the hard elements should be considered at a very early stage in the design process. The approach to a building and its setting in and response to the broader landscape around it are most likely to be the first impression a householder or visitor will have of a property. It will set the tone for what may be found inside and cannot therefore be considered as an optional extra, but rather as a major part of the whole concept. The space between buildings cannot also just be left to chance if the right impact is to be made. Professional help in this area (*see* Chapter 4) is very important for the uninitiated, as it is all too easy to make mistakes and choose the wrong plants, materials and style. Planning officers often impose enforceable requirements in planning approvals for landscaping and these usually have to be confirmed before the building work is started on site.

Many councils object to the suburbanization of rural conversion schemes and restrict garden areas and detailing so that courtyards, for example, are laid to gravel up to the walls of the surrounding buildings without hedges or fences dividing the space or delineating the boundaries.

Internal circulation can also often be located on the courtyard side of a conversion as an additional buffer space, allowing privacy in the main living and sleeping spaces.

Choice of hard landscaping materials should also reflect former uses and sometimes internal materials can be reclaimed for outdoor use, for example paviours from former stable blocks. Stone flags and bricks used for external paving can look attractive, but can suffer from frost damage in more exposed areas. The more absorbent materials have to be located carefully to avoid spalling and cracking.

EXTENSIONS

Conservatories or loggias also require careful consideration. If possible, they should be provided within the building shell by glazing sections of the roof and walls within the existing line, by cutting out a section of the original structure. In walled court situations simple 'lean-to' glasshouse extensions can look more appropriate than hipped or gabled versions. Detailing of ridges, eaves and windows should reflect the character of the existing building, as should the material chosen for the construction of the extension.

(Opposite) An unusual glazed extension that reflects the height and facets of the main building to which it is attached.
(Nigel Rigden)

CHAPTER 6

Detailed Design

SPACES

Living Areas

The main reason for choosing to convert an existing building is the prospect of acquiring a considerable amount of space at a reasonably affordable price. To enjoy and benefit from this space it is essential to employ the volume to good effect by revealing its individual characteristics, which in many cases should offer more than a hint of the previous use and the original structure of the building.

The presence of strong architectural features should dictate the distribution of the principal spaces, with the main living area usually taking priority. This can often mean that living spaces are on an upper level to take advantage of an interesting roof structure or to offer good views out across the surrounding countryside. An open mind regarding traditional living patterns may therefore be required with conversion projects, as unlike a new build there will be many fixed features to take into account. Amongst the most essential features for a living room is good natural daylight and the presence of existing openings may well dictate the position of the living space. Tall openings may, for instance, suggest a galleried space with split-level living accommodation.

OPPOSITE: This night shot clearly shows the galleried landing and double height space. (Nigel Rigden)

A living area can also be a main reception room, which links the main parts of the house. (Nigel Rigden)

To avoid corridors, the living area may need to be the principal reception space and the primary circulation route. This enables it to become the hub of the house and it is currently fashionable for this space to contain kitchen and breakfast areas. Stairways leading off this space can also add much interest to the room by opening up vertical space.

Fireplaces are traditionally thought of as focal points in main reception areas, but with conversions it is most unlikely that there will be an existing one. Therefore, if this option is being considered either to heat or to provide 'decoration', its location is crucial. Many planning departments object to new chimneys on barn or rural conversion projects where there was not one previously. If that is the case, the type of fire and fuel can be an important factor in determining the location of the fire and the structure of the room. The style of the fire will also influence the character of the room or space. For example, the choice of wood burners, efficient in usage and utilitarian in appearance, may complement a former industrial or agricultural building.

Kitchens

Many factors need to be considered when choosing the location of the kitchen area. Your own priorities should be set out to help with the decision if the location is not immediately obvious (although in the interest of security, it is often sensible to have the kitchen window overlooking the entrance to the property). The kitchen is now commonly used not only for food preparation, but also for eating and entertaining. It is usually best located close to the social hub of the home and on any convenient level to take advantage of existing openings and features.

Choice of style is not easy in a conversion. There is such a wide range of styles and finishes available that it may be more appropriate to choose a loose range of fittings rather than a rigid layout. This allows a degree of flexibility in trying to fit something contemporary that has rigid lines against possibly an old masonry wall, which will most likely be out of true both horizontally and vertically. Lining the walls may be the only solution to achieve a level background if fitted units are to be utilized.

A kitchen with a loose range of equipment.
(Nigel Rigden)

OPPOSITE: A wood-burning stove which is in keeping with the agricultural nature of the converted barn.
(Nigel Rigden)

A fitted kitchen with coordinated fixtures and fittings. (Nigel Rigden)

RIGHT: A kitchen shown complete with a 'range style' of cooker. (Nigel Rigden)

BELOW: A balanced flue terminal set in stonework. (Nigel Rigden)

The choice of cooking appliance is a major factor in the design of a kitchen. The space and volumes often encountered in properties for conversion lend themselves ideally to the constant and gentler background heat of a range style of cooker. These are now available in a variety of fuel types from wood through to bottle gas. A range also provides a strong focal point and a welcoming feature to sit nearby, helping to extend the function of the kitchen area. They can also provide central heating and hot water.

Utility room with separate external access.
(Nigel Rigden)

Conventional double oven cookers are also popular and avoid the need for a flue. They come in a variety of colours and by virtue of their size are in scale with many conversion projects. There is, however, considerable variety nowadays in the types of flue available. These options allow more flexibility in locating the cooking range and therefore the position of the kitchen. Balanced and fan-assisted flues are unobtrusive and can be located very close to the ground.

This flexibility overcomes the major problem of where to position the flue outlet. If solid fuel is the preferred option, then black-painted industrial metal flues are generally favoured over stone or brick chimneys, which are considered too domestic in character. This is a topic of much divided opinion and the local authority should be approached early in the design process.

An effective ventilation and extraction system is essential in a modern kitchen and the requirements and solutions are discussed later in the chapter.

Layout options will obviously depend on the space available, but it is most likely that the cooking area will be part of a much larger space. The visual definition of the work zone can be achieved by various methods. Disposition of the kitchen cupboards or units – such as island or peninsular arrangements or changes in floor finish or ceiling height – are amongst the most common ideas. Lighting can also be used to

subtle effect in unobtrusively defining cooking and eating areas.

Utility Areas

If natural daylight is at a premium through lack of existing openings or planning restrictions, then utility rooms can be sited within internal areas. However, utility areas are most commonly linked with boot rooms, which are adjacent to the garden or driveway delivery access – the back door. It is therefore not essential for the kitchen to be adjacent to the driveway or garage for deliveries. Utility areas often double as drying rooms with the boiler, washing machine and tumble dryer conveniently located near the outside drying yard. Pets can also have their baskets in the utility room with cat flaps in the external door.

Bedrooms

Space for bedrooms can be allocated anywhere there is natural light and ventilation provided there is a means of escape to the outside, preferably without passing through the main living area. The whole family should be involved and consulted at all stages of the detail design period so that preferences and priorities are taken into consideration to determine room layouts. If the project is designed for full-time occupation by the family, then the priorities are likely to be different to those of a holiday home conversion.

Master bedrooms require a large amount of space, as they now tend to be part of a suite of rooms with a dressing room and en suite bathroom included. These can be separated from the remaining sleeping accommodation, especially if there is a maturing family sharing the home. This can help to avoid uneconomic extended circulation space by, for instance, locating the master bedroom one side of the living area and the remaining family and guest rooms on the other. Generous space for a variety of bed types and sizes should always be allowed with plenty of room for bedside cabinets and lights either side of double beds or between twin beds. Adequate power sockets and environmental controls should be located readily to hand. The position of television and telephone points should also be carefully considered, as well as good levels of light for dressing and reading areas.

An example of a spacious master bedroom. (Nigel Rigden)

Roof or attic spaces can accommodate sleeping areas with low zones adjacent to the eaves either filled with storage units or covered to match the remainder to give an illusion of space. These loft spaces can be ideal children's rooms, where height is not so critical, and where they will be able to live away from the remainder of the house. They can be given a degree of independence not always attainable in the body of a traditional house. Space for desks for homework and computers is now essential in children's rooms and robust construction of floors and walls will help to keep noise levels from the latest CD or DVD player or musical instrument to acceptable levels.

In listed buildings, the Conservation Office may dictate how space can be divided within a conversion project. To maintain an historic structure it may not be possible to create cellular space for all the normal activities associated with usual household living. For example, it might be necessary to allocate open gallery space for sleeping, possibly without separation from the main body of the building, which could ultimately restrict the use of the conversion to occasional or holiday stays. This type of restriction, however, could also suggest a layout with bedrooms on the lower level and living rooms overhead.

Division of bedrooms can also be made flexible by movable partitioning so that dormitory layouts can be accommodated when entertaining groups or young visitors.

If attic space is utilized and roof lights only are permitted by the planners, then means of escape in the event of fire has to be considered and the Building Regulations Part B will apply (*see* Chapter 2). Special-sized top-hung escape windows are manufactured for this situation, and should be installed in accordance with the Regulations and located not more than 1.7m from the eaves of the roof.

Bathrooms

Locating sanitary accommodation is not always easy in a large space, as it can be difficult to be unobtrusive with small volumes. Ingenuity is therefore required to lose or disguise these small intrusions into often very large spaces. Furthermore, the new disabled access regulations require a WC being provided on the entrance level of the building.

The provision of natural light and ventilation can be a problem if appropriate existing openings are not available or have been utilized in other spaces. Locating waste pipes also has to be carefully considered, as they are not always appropriate externally, although unobtrusive ductwork can help to disguise them internally. There is a legal requirement to avoid the noise nuisance of flushing and draining water, so it is helpful if soil downpipes are wrapped in sound-deadening quilt, especially if they have to pass through living rooms.

En suite arrangements are now common where the bathing area is located off a bedroom. These are not necessarily partitioned, but rather zoned with low-

An en suite bathroom can take up little space.
(Nigel Rigden)

screening modesty dividers combined with a good extractor system.

Wet rooms are now becoming increasingly popular here, although they have been common in many overseas countries for some time. Central floor gullies with gentle falls from the perimeter of the wet room allow for sluicing down and the shower area can be included without a separate tray and enclosure. This can give freedom of movement and easy access in otherwise confined spaces. Shallow floor gullies allow these rooms to be installed in many parts of the conversion, as longer, gentle falls on the waste pipes are more achievable.

Studies (The Home Office)

Working from home and the use of computers for more and more household tasks mean that study areas are also increasingly being provided in new homes and conversions. They should preferably be soundproofed to allow homework, for instance, to proceed undistracted, or if they are to be used for

An en suite dressing room with fitted clothes storage cupboards. (Nigel Rigden)

A simple and functional bathroom. (Nigel Rigden)

BELOW: An example of a 'wet floor' type of shower room, where wastewater is allowed to drain to a floor gully. The floor, walls and ceiling are completely tiled. (Nigel Rigden)

visiting clients. They should also ideally be off the entrance area if business visitors are expected frequently; nor should they be too far from beverage-making facilities.

They may be sited away from views if classed as secondary accommodation, but if considered the most important room in the conversion and in constant use then a prime location will have to be found. They can also be designated areas off the main living or circulation space, perhaps utilizing a large landing area, although this can cause disturbance to those using the space. A dividing screen doubling as a storage unit can give visual separation.

Storage

Storage space is always at a premium, but with many conversions the loft space may be left open to the living rooms, thus depriving the house of one of the most frequently used storage areas. However, when converting a large building there should be ample opportunity to build in more than adequate storage space. Use of 'thick' walls, a minimum of 600mm apart between rooms, is one successful and

This storage was built in as part of a wall. (Nigel Rigden)

unobtrusive method of creating storage space without destroying the geometry of the adjoining room.

If storage is created in semi-basement areas, possibly against retaining walls and utilizing areas that have no external wall openings, it is essential to keep these areas dry and well ventilated. Still pockets of air can lead to heavy mould growth, which will damage stored items. Likewise, under-stair voids can also be successfully utilized, but again need to be provided with ventilation and positive air movement to avoid stale air.

If roof voids are utilized for storage, ceiling joists often require strengthening to allow for the load imposed upon them. There are various of ways of doing this, from adding new timber joists between the existing ones or introducing steelwork. The building inspector, however, will require structural calculations to prove the structure is adequate for the purpose you propose.

Workshops

Workshops are usually associated with garaging and other externally accessed accommodation. Nevertheless, workshop and hobby rooms are required increasingly for the early retired and those with serious hobbies. These will need to be spacious, well lit and warm. Basements lend themselves very well to this type of workshop, because they can be left untidy after use and they are well away from the remainder of the property for purposes of acoustic separation. If

A modern light fitting, which contrasts very effectively with the industrial timber framework. (Nigel Rigden)

OPPOSITE: Spot lighting has been used to highlight roof timbers. (Nigel Rigden)

heavy loads have to be hoisted the use of the existing structure should be approached with great care. Old industrial buildings, however, lend themselves well to this type of use as they often have very strong floors. Likewise, a good extractor system may be required if engines are to be tested while running or if other industrial processes are involved.

BUILDING SERVICES

Lighting

Lighting a conversion project can mean the introduction of an element into the building that was not previously present – this gives a great opportunity to devise a well-considered scheme using lighting to enhance the character of the building and highlight features not found in conventional domestic buildings, such as an old beam or roof truss.

There are professional lighting consultants available to help with advice on choosing the right fittings and the right levels of light and hue and how best to achieve this. Concealed light sources can be designed into the scheme with the necessary wiring circuits put in place before partitions and floors have been completed. It is also very important to conceal services in sensitive locations, such as in chapel conversions or buildings of historic importance.

Low-voltage downlighters have become very popular, as they are unobtrusive and very bright, especially when recessed. However, recessed lights in

107

a ceiling void will often require fireproofing hoods to maintain the integrity of the fire rating between the floors. The building inspector will advise on this aspect. All low-voltage systems require a transformer and its position is important. If it is attached to the track, it can be lumpy and difficult to conceal. Some fittings have individual transformers, which makes them larger but disguises the bulk of the transformers. Central transformers for up to six lights are large and are best concealed in roof voids or cupboards, although they cannot be too remote from the fittings they control.

Track lighting is more flexible and avoids the fireproofing requirement, making it an effective way of reducing costs while maintaining standards. The use of dimmer switches gives the option of variety and mood lighting.

Wall-mounted uplighters can be painted in to match the wall to help reduce their impact; they can be used to illuminate the roof structure and wall textures above. Local light sources will usually be required to supplement uplighters and a separate 5amp lighting circuit switched remotely could well control these. This avoids the use of intensive central pendant lighting, which may be inappropriate in the reception rooms in a conversion.

Heating and Ventilation

This is a specialist field and it is about the most critical installation in terms of your future enjoyment of the property. If the heating and ventilation system is

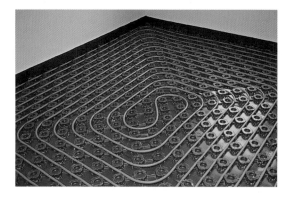

Underfloor piped hot-water heating system.
(Nigel Rigden)

thoughtfully designed and everything works as planned, it will provide a comfortable environment in which to live. If, after commissioning, it goes wrong and leaves the building without heat and water you are likely to be most unhappy!

On the larger project, it could be very worthwhile employing a building services engineer (*see* Chapter 4). He will design a system to your requirements, although the type of heating system chosen will partly depend on what fuel is available locally. Suitably qualified contractors, however, can design and price less complicated schemes quite effectively.

Many rural areas are without natural gas supplies and you will need to consider the most cost-effective alternatives as these can vary according to fluctuating oil, bottle gas and electricity prices. With the Building Regulations on insulation standards being frequently upgraded, the resultant cost of space heating is now often lower than that of operating household appliances.

It is also now increasingly popular for wet underfloor heating systems to be installed, which avoids the need for radiators and provides a gentle background heat. This can, of course, be supplemented by open fires, provided that chimneys are permitted or they already exist. A conventional wet radiator system can then be used as back-up heating on the first and subsequent floor levels, with the main floor acting as a giant storage heater. The property should then be thoroughly warmed throughout.

Underfloor heating can also be installed within timber floors, although it requires very careful detailing of the insulation and floor covering. The system manufacturer will specify exactly how it can be installed in these situations and it is advisable to use only certificated engineers approved by the manufacturer to carry out these installations.

Ventilation legislation is becoming increasingly onerous, largely to ensure that new buildings have airtight construction with a minimum standard of controlled air movement (*see* Chapter 2). Part F of the Regulations stipulates the amount of area of free ventilation for each room. Background ventilation to all living rooms is required and is now usually achieved by integral ventilators in the heads of external windows and doors.

Some of the mortar joints between ridge tiles have been left out to provide roof ventilation. (Barrie Davies)

Bathrooms, kitchens and utility rooms additionally require extractor fans, with the Regulations laying down the rate of air extraction in litres per second. The manufacturers of extractor fans produce good literature on the best way of complying with the Regulations. Some extractors are controlled by a humidistat to alleviate the risk of condensation and subsequent possible mould growth.

Ventilation of roof voids to avoid condensation is required and can be achieved by proprietary ridge and eave ventilators. It is also now common practice to utilize breathable roofing felts to allow air movement through the membrane, thus avoiding the need for additional vents. The building inspector may also have a view on the right solution.

Open fires, boilers and stoves for cooking/heating require natural ventilation for combustion. The size of the appliance needs to be related strictly to the free area of the ventilation grille that is to be utilized. Gas fires and boilers in particular are governed by CORGI (the Council for Registered Gas Installers) and only approved and qualified contractors are allowed to carry out installation work. The position of ventilation and extraction grilles needs to be considered early in the project. These aspects do not want to be expressed obtrusively on the outside of the building or left to chance for an insensitive engineer to put them where it is most convenient. Roof ventilators are readily available in a variety of materials,

which makes them barely detectable in the line of the roof slope.

MAINS SERVICES

Water

It is quite common that buildings deemed suitable for conversion are simple stores or animal buildings lacking any mains services. The proximity of a mains water supply is often a major selling point if the building is being advertised prior to conversion. Remote barns, whilst a very attractive prospect for conversion, may well not have any mains service, and

An existing chimney of a former school has been reused and given a new flue liner and terminal. (Barrie Davies)

Examples of aluminium rainwater pipes and guttering. The sections are traditional and when painted are hard to tell apart from the original cast-iron gutters and downpipes that they replace. (Nigel Rigden)

so the connection charges can amount to a considerable percentage of the overall cost of the project. Water companies provide the polythene mains pipework and have to carry out the connection work on any new main. Only their approved contractors can undertake road excavation work, so these two items are somewhat out of the developer's control.

Many remoter buildings rely on a private supply, which can provide good quality water but may require regular analysis to check on quality. It may also tend to dry up in drought conditions.

In less remote areas, gas may also be available and this can share a trench with the water main. Occasionally, the electricity supply and the telephone may also share this trench and the Highways Department as well as the service providers have a standard approach to the approved arrangement and separation of the four services. This, of course, removes the need for unsightly overhead lines, but if distances are too great and trenching too expensive then overhead lines may be the only option open to you. In conservation areas though, overhead lines may not be allowed, so there is no choice but to use trenching. If in doubt, it is best to check this with the area Planning Authority.

Drainage

With the increasing incidence of flooding throughout the country, drainage is now an important and sometimes complex issue to resolve. Many remote farm buildings and especially water mills can find themselves in a water catchment area that is monitored and controlled by the Environment Agency. In these circumstances, depending on the geology of the site or the high-water table, it may not be possible to discharge effluent into a septic tank with a filter bed for any surplus overflow. In this situation, a cesspit will have to be provided with access for a commercial vehicle to empty the container on a regular basis. The size and location of the cesspit will have to be established by taking into consideration the nature of the land, the total number of people served and access to the pit. Proprietary underground tanks are available from several manufacturers with a range of sizes and shapes.

If septic tanks are permitted, then location and subsoil type are critical, as percolation rates have to be tested and tabulated for Water Authority approval. These can take a considerable time to monitor if clay is present, as percolation can take several hours or even days if the ground is already saturated. The results will establish the size and type of tank and filter bed, which will then have to be approved by the statutory authority, often as a condition of the planning consent.

Reed beds are one environmentally friendly approach to this problem and have been used successfully in suitable locations. The Centre for Alternative Technology at Machynlleth is one source of information on this and many other innovative energy and resource conservation ideas.

Surface water disposal is not usually such a sensitive issue as foul water, although in a new installation surface and foul water are not permitted to be combined in the same drain. It is usually possible either to connect rainwater pipes and gullies to the existing system or to construct soakaway pits at a reasonable distance from the property. Use of permeable materials externally, such as gravel rather than tarmac, will allow percolation without concentrating surface water, thus avoiding its disposal elsewhere.

Land drains that are used to relieve water pressure from retaining walls or to divert water around properties are frequently encountered and should be kept on a separate system and preferably taken to an existing watercourse.

The style, type and colour of rainwater goods are a very important external design feature. Often, old farm buildings will have been neglected, and their rainwater goods will have long since disappeared, or there will be none available to match those that remain. Planning authorities often stipulate what can be used if the building is of architectural merit; this is most likely to be cast iron or aluminium equivalents and not UPVC. Long term, this is the best solution but it does add considerably to the cost. Large ranges of gutter and downpipe sections are available, but for simple buildings, traditional unfussy styles are most appropriate and, preferably, those using rafter brackets or spiked to walls rather introducing fascia boards.

ENERGY CONSERVATION

This issue is increasingly important and legislation under the Part L of the Building Regulations is now largely directed towards conservation of fossil fuels

The windows of this former school form part of the listing and as such cannot be effectively double-glazed without resort to secondary glazing. (Barrie Davies)

(*see* Chapter 2). High levels of insulation and energy efficiency are now mandatory on all projects. This can prove costly, but those with the means and philosophy to help reduce emissions, in the long term, can still usually improve basic standards without great additional initial outlay.

Insulation

Examples of successful energy-conserving projects are now well-documented, but in some conversion projects it will prove impossible to reconcile architectural features with energy conservation measures. In these circumstances it may be possible to trade off elements of structure that cannot be altered by improving insulation values where the additional material or thickness to achieve this are not noticeable, such as within the roof structure or under the floor. It may not be possible or desirable to double-glaze windows of special interest or construction, particularly in church or school conversions. A good relationship with Building Control inspectors is essential; many are prepared to be constructive in cases where the conventional route is not feasible.

Floors are now required to be insulated, possibly needing up to 150mm of rigid foam board below the finished ground-floor level. With underfloor heating systems it can take 300–350mm to construct a new floor, depending on floor finish. If ceiling or beam heights are low, this will require excavation below the existing floor to achieve a reasonable new ceiling height. Excavation, incidentally, can reveal the depth and condition of footings, if any, on the adjoining outside walls, and may well indicate if any underpinning is required, particularly if increased loading is proposed by a change of use.

Walls may require insulation to be installed, depending on the overall condition and opportunity for upgrading the remainder of the property. Thermal board, insulation-bonded to the rear of plasterboard dry lining, is the most common and cost-effective method of achieving this. It is fixed to the masonry walls after they have been damp-proofed, either mechanically or on plaster dabs, then finished to suit the remainder of the property. This system also allows an opportunity for service drops to be made without chasing the masonry walls.

This window of a former watermill had to be restored to its original condition. Double-glazing was not permitted. (Nigel Rigden)

Roofs can be more difficult to insulate in a conversion project, as the added thickness of some insulation boards can push the roof finishes beyond the line of the existing masonry on gables. Careful thought therefore needs to be given to the position of the insulation and its relationship to any existing timbers that may be retained and left exposed. This is when 'warm roof' construction is used, whereby the insulation is at roof level rather than at ceiling level, leaving the attic space above uninsulated.

There are some thin foil and foam sandwich insulation products designed for the aircraft industry that lend themselves well to conversion projects due to their flexibility and high levels of thermal performance. They do, however, require a double layer of timber battens to allow condensation to drain down the roof into the gutters.

If roofs are being rebuilt, insulation boards are available that are designed to fit between the rafters. If possible, this is a sensible approach as labour costs are thereby kept to a minimum.

ACOUSTICS

As noted earlier, open-plan living can be very difficult to reconcile with good acoustic separation, and this aspect of the project has to be carefully considered early on in the design stage. Part E of the Building Regulations requires acoustic separation, to an acceptable standard, *between rooms* and all the proposed measures that are to be taken to reduce noise have to be included with the application for approval (*see* Chapter 2). By zoning apart the quiet and noisy areas in a passive way and using new or existing masonry walls, much of the problem can be overcome without costly remedies.

STRUCTURE

It is general planning policy that buildings considered worthy of conversion should be structurally sound and of traditional or vernacular construction. The successful conversion will exploit the major characteristics of the original and tailor the new use to the existing structure rather than moulding the raw material into something at odds with it.

Residential conversion is generally considered the most difficult to reconcile with traditional agricul-

tural buildings. It is necessary to transform the large areas of wall and internal volumes under uninterrupted roofs of what was usually a store into a building type consisting of small cellular spaces reflecting the differing functions of living, eating, sleeping and bathing.

Farm buildings that were used to house animals in winter usually had the feed stored on strongly built floors over the animals' heads so that it could be easily dropped down into their troughs. These buildings in particular can translate into accommodation with an open living area over cellular sleeping space. This can allow elements of the existing floor structure to be utilized as well as retaining the complete roof structure. Principal roof trusses and purlins are often substantial enough to be retained with only the decayed or warped elements replaced, thereby maintaining the simple characteristics of the original structure.

In barns, the openings in the stone walls are traditionally the access doorways, with some ventilation

No new openings were permitted in this barn conversion. This restricted the internal planning to having to relate to the existing openings in the gable elevation. (Barrie Davies)

slots. Planning offices are reluctant to allow new openings to be formed, preferring to encourage the retention of large areas of uninterrupted wall. Any new windows that are allowed should maintain the original character of the building and will normally be purpose-made to reflect existing construction details.

Access openings or cart doors can be fully glazed satisfactorily and if recessed can also help to light separate spaces internally.

Original lintel, arch and quoin features can also be utilized effectively for new openings, although large openings are often more in keeping with the scale of the original building; several small openings have a tendency to indicate 'conversion', rather than remaining true to the spirit of the original.

OPPOSITE: The large opening on this elevation replaces almost exactly the original one used as access for large machinery. (Nigel Rigden)

ABOVE: Vertical timber slats, with glazing behind, have replaced the old access door on this barn. This gives the impression that the barn door is still in place. (Barrie Davies)

The original orchard has helped to retain the character and setting of this barn. (Nigel Rigden)

This landscaping reflects the rural origins by retaining an ancient ash tree and by the introduction of 'country' stone walls. (Nigel Rigden)

EXTERNAL DESIGN

The careful treatment of the space between and around conversion buildings is a very important consideration and is commonly the subject of planning conditions. The overall project should be considered in its entirety both inside and out and related harmoniously to its context, whether in the open countryside, or a village or urban setting. For instance, the retention or replanting of orchards, together with a careful choice of native trees and shrubs, can help to soften and integrate farm buildings in their transformation from agricultural to domestic usage.

The site plan drawing should illustrate the landscaping proposals and relate them to the internal arrangement of rooms so that aspect and exposure are considered when deciding the final layout of accommodation and external access points. Walling, preferably brick, stone or natural hedging with common local species, should ideally define boundaries.

However, it is not always appropriate to define boundaries. For instance, in the case of groups of buildings, several small gardens would be at odds with the scale and character of the original open farmyard layout, so open courts are encouraged.

This entrance is bold and unfussy, in keeping with the original farmyard access. (Nigel Rigden)

In both industrial and agricultural conversions, it is important to retain external features that allude to the original function of the building such as mill wheels, dovecots and troughs.

Orchards and ponds are also characteristics of the countryside that are now scarce, partly due to intense farming practices. Yard areas for clothes drying and garden implement stores also have to be considered carefully. If old granaries or cart sheds are available for storage they should be utilized. Walled areas can conceal the more mundane features such as bin and fuel stores. Materials for surfacing should also be selected carefully, with gravels and pavings used in preference to tarmac or brick paviours.

Likewise, vehicle parking should ideally be inconspicuous and screened by buildings or walling. Open cart sheds can also readily be chosen to echo barn and stable doors, rather than modern alternatives. Entrance areas should be understated, with visibility splays and hardened access driveways kept to a minimum. If possible, the original entrance should be retained to avoid loss of hedging and the need to introduce Highways Department standards.

SECURITY AND LIGHTING

Householders are now encouraged to take security precautions more seriously – for example, in some areas police may not attend scenes of minor burglaries if their published advice has not been implemented. On the other hand, especially in rural areas, the police force can easily become overstretched.

The local police force will probably have an architectural liaison officer to implement 'secured by design' principles at the planning stage of any project. The officer will normally respond to a set of plans and schedule of works and will assess the likely risk of a particular location based on crime records. A telephone call could avoid unnecessary expense and suggest the most effective way of combating potential burglaries. Whole-house security systems are now increasingly common, and there are many highly reputable and efficient companies offering design and installation services. Recommendations or references are strongly advised and regular maintenance or testing is essential, so reputable local companies should be invited to provide an estimate for the installation.

With a conversion, the normal option of choosing where to site a new build project is obviously not available, so compromises may have to be made with regard to security. Landscaping can be designed to avoid blind spots. Boundary fencing and gates should be specified correctly and the right ironmongery chosen for both gates and stores, especially for sheds and garages. Insurance companies will also specify what security fittings are required for windows and doors, particularly final exit doors. Their advice should be seen as a minimum standard only and additional security considered.

External lighting is an added deterrent, and there is an enormous range of passive infrared (PIR) fittings available. Advice should be sought on both what size of lamp is required and where the fittings should be located for maximum effect. If you have neighbours, however, avoid pointing lights at their windows, as they can cause nuisance and give rise to official complaint. Maintenance should also be considered as the lamps require periodic renewal; if they are located very high up it can be difficult for maintenance to be carried out without employing an installation engineer.

CHAPTER 7

Specifications, Tenders and Contracts

'The difficulty about a gentlemen's agreement is that it depends on the continued existence of the gentlemen.'
(Reginald Withers Payne, Judge of the High Court)

CONTRACT DOCUMENTS

No one would consider baking a cake without a recipe comprising a complete list of ingredients and details of preparation or without any idea of what it is going to look like. Likewise, you should not consider carrying out major building works without a specification, a comprehensive set of working drawings and some form of contract. These are known as contract documents.

It is unfortunate that the most common type of civil dispute occurs between builders and their clients. This is possibly the result of muddled communication, misunderstanding and the lack of a formal contract. Contractors have a tendency, in the absence of a contract and comprehensive specifications and drawings, to make assumptions, which may or may not be to your liking. Also clients have a mistaken belief that what is in their mind is clearly understood by the contractor. This is where professionals are better able to translate your ideas into a set of contract documents, which are clearly understood by contractors and leave little room for misunderstanding and conflict. Specifications, drawings and a contract are therefore essential information to ensure that your wishes have been formalized and can be properly realized. Your architect will usually prepare these as part of his normal services (*see* Chapter 4).

It is crucial that sufficient time is allowed in the overall programme to prepare comprehensive contract documents. If the process is rushed, then items may be inadvertently forgotten; for any items that have not been fully specified provisional cost allowances will need to be made. The problem of having too many provisional costs or sums, known as provisional sums (PS sums) or prime costs (PC sums), is that the contractor does not have to price them until they are expended during the works on site. This makes for uncertainty, and allows the contractor to submit prices in excess of the original PS or PC sums, especially if any of these sums were inadequate.

WORKING DRAWINGS

Working drawings, or more properly constructional drawings, will generally consist of plans of each floor, all elevations and a number of cross sections through the building to show how various levels relate. A typical section would include any basement and roof space. These drawings are produced to a scale of 1:100 and 1:50 depending on the size of the building and complexity of the works proposed. A 1:100 scale drawing is normally sufficient for elevations, but plans and sections would be drawn at 1:50 in order that more detail can be shown. These drawings are also the ones that form the basis of the application for Building Regulations Approval and are useful for submission to building societies when applying for finance.

Other drawings, which can form part of the set, are constructional details where the scale of the normal plans is not sufficient to show clear details of how things are to be constructed, such as windows, foundations and stairs. They are produced at various scales such as 1:20, 1:10 and 1:5, or even larger if there is a great need for clarity.

Most architects today use computer-aided drawing systems (CAD) to produce working drawings and programs, such as *AutoCAD*®. These have

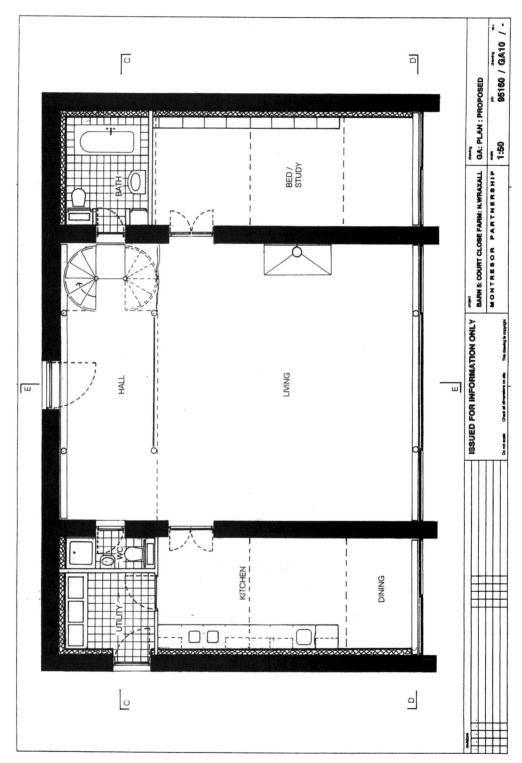

A typical plan drawn at 1:50 scale shows the arrangement of spaces and fixtures. Note the insulation to the walls (wavy lines).
(Montresor Partnership)

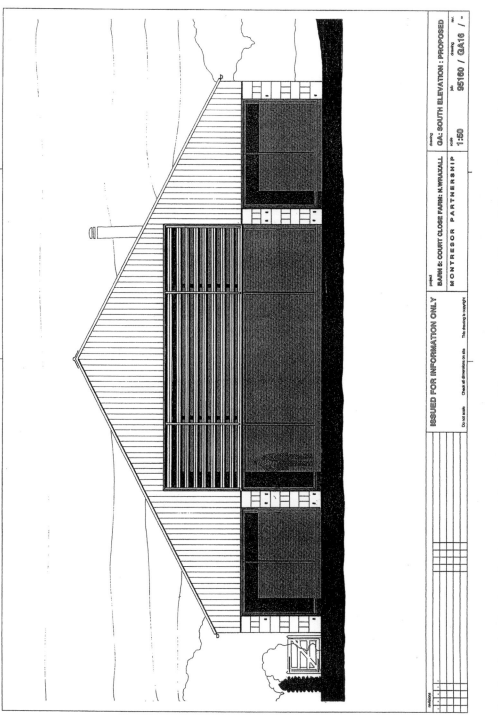

An elevation drawing showing what is proposed (see the main view of the converted cart barn in Chapter 9 for how the proposal turned out). (Montresor Partnership)

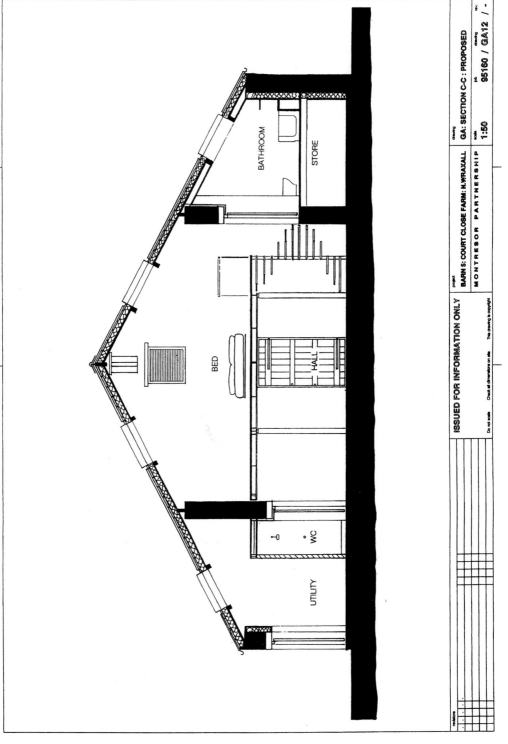

A sectional drawing showing the vertical arrangements of rooms and heights. (Montresor Partnership)

revolutionized the way information is set out on drawings and the ability to make changes and alterations. Drawings can also be shared with other professionals by simply making a copy on disc, which can be downloaded and used as a template to add specialist information such as structural details or positions of services This saves time and money, as the drawings have only to be produced once. It also maintains accuracy as everyone is working from the same base drawings. However, there are less complicated drawing packages that a non-professional can use to good effect. These are relatively inexpensive and if you have a PC it may be worthwhile trying one out. It may help with formulating the brief and in discussions with the local authority.

SPECIFICATION

A specification is a written document set out in accordance with a standard format. The specification usually describes in detail the work that has to be carried out, the types and qualities of materials to be used and standards of workmanship. The architect will prepare the specification, but on larger projects a quantity surveyor is also usually appointed to produce a 'Bill of Quantities' (*see* Chapter 4). The specification (or 'Bill') is the document actually priced by the contractor and it is where checks can be made as to the authenticity of the individual prices submitted.

There are numerous books available on writing specifications; some architects on larger projects use the standard headings and clauses produced by the National Building Specification (NBS). This is a common arrangement of work sections, which is compatible with the various forms of contract, British Standards and the Standard Method of Measurement (SMM) used by most quantity surveyors.

A typical specification for minor works consists of a schedule divided into headings, or work sections, which are then divided into subsections with relevant clauses. Dependent on the nature of the proposed works, some of the headings will be needed while others may not. The following headings are taken from the standard NBS specification and will give you an indication of what is covered.

1. **Preliminaries and General Conditions** This is normally the largest section and will contain the particulars of the project, for example, the names and addresses of all the parties involved and if appropriate their representatives. It will also describe the site and the existing buildings and give a brief description of the works to be carried out. It will include reference to materials to be supplied and work to be carried out by yourself or others. The form of contract to be used is normally confirmed along with any amendments. There will also be clauses on the tendering procedure and a list of the tender drawings. There will be reference to the management of the works, for example insurance provision, programme and valuations.

2. **Demolition, Alteration and Removal** The works to be included here are known as 'spot' items and any clauses will describe specific operations involving many trades, for example, removing parts of the building, cutting openings, stripping out services and making good and so on. This section can also specify specialist treatments such as eradication of beetle infestation and fungus (wet and dry rot) and any specialist decontamination.

3. **Groundwork** This section will include clauses relating to excavation and backfilling. Other clauses will deal with trenches for services, pipe ducts and the bedding of pipes.

4. **Concrete** This section will relate to in situ and pre-cast concrete. There will be clauses on the appropriate mixes for concrete, its handling, placing and protection. There will be clauses on formwork, reinforcement and surface finish.

5. **Masonry and Brickwork** This section describes walling in general and will contain clauses describing the bricks and blocks to be used and where, the types of mortar and the profile of the joints. Other clauses will describe any natural stone and how it is to be used and where. There will be clauses on the formation of cavities, cavity insulation, wall ties and damp-proof courses. There will be a section on pre-cast concrete sills, lintels and copings. Also there will be a reference to prefabricated steel lintels.

6. **Structural Steelwork and Timberwork** Here, any structural steelwork members are described, for example simple beams and joists. Their surface treatment and installation will be specified. The remainder of the section will cover the quality, strength and installation of timber joists, roof purlins and rafters. Also covered will be the selection of timber and any preservative treatment.

7. **Claddings and Roof Coverings** This section will describe external sheet claddings and their installation, for example timber weatherboarding. Also there will be a section on clay and concrete roof tiles and their installation. There will be clauses on the underlay, battens and detailing of eaves, valleys and so on. A section will be necessary for natural or artificial slate. There will also be reference to the treatment of existing roof tiling.

8. **Waterproofing** Here, liquid and flexible sheet damp-proofing membranes (DPMs) are described along with clauses on their installation. Also this is where built-up felt roof coverings will be described. There will be clauses on the decking, insulation, vapour control, chippings and so on. The repair of existing coverings will also be described if appropriate.

9. **Partitions and Linings** The new construction and repair of plasterboard dry lining systems will be described, including the finishing of joints and gaps. The materials to be used and installation of chipboard and timber board flooring will also be described.

10. **Windows**, **Doors and Stairs** There will be a section on the specification of timber, aluminium and UPVC windows and roof lights. The glazing details in general and any specialist finish or treatment will be described. Doors and shutters will be described and whether they are to be purpose- made or are to come from a proprietary manufacturer. If any are to be fire-resisting, the correct British or European Standard will need to be quoted. Any new timber stairway will be described with clauses on the balustrade, handrail and finish. Metal spiral stairs including fire-escape stairs would also be described here.

11. **Surface Finishes** This can be quite a large section, which deals with the numerous types of finish available. Here, floor screeds will be described along with rendered and plastered coatings. The composition of them, materials to be used and application are described including any water-proofing additives. New work will be described along with any repairs to existing screeds, renders and plasterwork. Wall and floor tiling is described regarding installation and material, for example stone, quarry or ceramic. The size of tile is to be specified along with bedding material, joint width and grouting. The type of sheet covering is to be specified, for example vinyl, cork or carpet. Any preparation, adhesives and underlays required are described and reference is made to any dampness present prior to the finishes being laid. Decorative papers and fabrics, if appropriate, can be specified along with paint, clear varnishes and stains. The painting clauses will include surface preparation and filling, the use of the appropriate primers, the number of undercoats and topcoats. There will be clauses on painting any existing previously decorated surfaces.

12. **Fixtures and Fittings**: This section will contain items such as specialized joinery, kitchen units, solid-fuel room heaters and so on. It will also contain the types, specification and numbers of the sanitary fittings to be included in the project, such as WCs, sinks, washbasins and showers. This section may also contain clauses detailing sizes, quality and fixing of skirtings, architraves, window boards, shelving and duct casings and so on.

13. **Insulation and Building Fabric** This is the section that deals with energy conservation and sound insulation. The legal requirements for such insulation are constantly being revised upwards and great care is required to ensure that what is specified meets the current regulations (*see* Chapter 2). This section will have clauses dealing with types and locations of insulating materials, such as within the loft, within wall cavities and between walls and floors. Within this section there is an opportunity to add clauses relating to the cutting of holes,

chases and the supports for services. Essentially, the requirements are such that holes and chases do not compromise the structural stability or sound resistance of the building, for example notches in floor joists, deep horizontal chases or large holes around service entries.

14. **External Works** There will be sections on kerbing and paving. The types of materials – such as stone, concrete, cobbles or brick – will be specified, including instructions on their laying and the thickness and types of the bedding materials and any foundation. Macadam pavings will be specified if appropriate and clauses will indicate the number of layers, their thickness and how they are to be laid and edged. Any fencing and gates will be specified as to height, line and support. There will be clauses, for instance, on setting any posts in concrete and on the construction of certain types of fencing, for example chain link, wooden post and rail, close boarding or wooden palisade. There may also be a requirement for clauses on benches, planters and play equipment.

15. **Drainage** This section will deal with rainwater pipework and gutters. There are clauses for either aluminium or plastic systems including their installation. Foul drainage above ground is specified using UPVC systems installed to British Standards. Drainage below ground allows for specification of either clay or UPVC pipes. There will be clauses on protection of and connection into existing drains, excavating pipe trenches, materials for bedding pipes and installation of fittings such as traps and gullies. There will be clauses on the construction of inspection chambers (manholes), and whether these are to be in brick or plastic. There will also be clauses on constructing channels and benching within the inspection chamber and on the cover and frame. If appropriate, there may be clauses on the construction of soakaways, septic tanks and cesspits. Notes on testing drainage systems will always need to be included.

16. **Piped Supplies** This section sets out the requirements for the hot and cold water systems. There will be clauses on what appliances are to be supplied and on the requirement to install the system in accordance with British Standards. There will be a description of the hot-water storage system and whether it is to be open vented or unvented. There should be notes on whether there are any local water heaters and instantaneous shower units. The cold-water storage cistern, if required, should be specified as to material and capacity. All fixings, positions, sizes and materials of pipes vents, overflow pipes and valves are to be specified, including the water service main. Insulation to pipes and cisterns will be specified. There will be a clause on how the system should be tested and notes that the installation of any gas main should comply with the gas service provider's requirements.

17. **Heating Systems** A brief description of the proposed system will be required detailing the heat source, heat circulation and heat emitters. There will be a requirement to specify basic design temperatures and provide heat loss calculations (U Values). There should be notes on what system controls are required. The specification of the fuel store will need to be confirmed, for example whether it is to be for oil or coal. There will be clauses on the treatment of any new or existing flue and air supply to any heat-emitting appliance. There will also be clauses on the specification of equipment such as radiators, valves, pumps and pipework, and details of system testing.

18. **Electric Power and Lighting** Details of the required circuits will need to be confirmed – kitchen, bedrooms, immersion heater and so on. All necessary conduits, fittings and types of cable and fixing will be specified, along with installation instructions and relevant British Standards. Any electrical accessories required, such as wall lights, sockets, shaver points and fused spurs, will be indicated. The position for the consumer unit and mains entry will be indicated. Any intruder or fire alarm and any access control will be specified, as well as connections for telecom equipment. A clause will be included requiring testing to be carried out in accordance with IEE Regulations (Institutution of Electrical Engineers).

'SIGN OFF'

The importance of formally approving the scheme, as specified and drawn by the architect, cannot be overemphasized. Most people are a bit put off by a set of drawings and a specification. They will only skim through what has been presented and it is often the case that they feel awkward in asking what to them may feel like silly questions. Drawings and specifications, to the inexperienced, are difficult to understand, but a good architect will take the time to go through them with you in order to ensure that they represent what you have requested.

This is the last realistic time to make any changes to the project, as at this point it is only a matter of altering a few drawings or editing the specification in the word processor. This is a crucial stage – once you have 'signed off' the drawings and specification and accepted a price from a builder, any subsequent changes, especially during construction, will normally cost you extra money!

BUILDING WORK PROCUREMENT

There are several routes that can be taken to carry out the conversion of your property and some of the most popular are detailed below.

Self-Build

Self-build is a route only for the experienced and for those who have sufficient time. This method can save up to 20 per cent on normal building costs, but you will need to work very hard to achieve your saving. You will be taking on the traditional role of a general building contractor. You will need to: purchase and store some of the materials; hire specialist subcontractors and dovetail their activities; provide labour for fetching, carrying and cleaning; and also undertake some of the construction work yourself. If you are employed, then you will have to do all of this whilst still working, concentrating on the project only in your spare time. This can be impossible for some and furthermore some employers will not tolerate any distraction and loss of performance during working hours. This will severely restrict your ability to manage and deal with emergencies. You cannot expect to do everything at evenings and weekends. If, however, you have the freedom and the time, it is a very good option.

Managed Subcontractors

This method is similar to self-build, except that you are hiring subcontractors to carry out all the work and quite possibly to supply the materials as well. You will still have to coordinate the project and ensure that there are no grey areas of responsibility. The process is quite time-consuming, as you need each subcontractor to visit the site with you and go through the proposed work. This needs to be done several times if you want competitive quotations. Always get quotations in writing and be clear as to what is being provided and what is not, such as scaffolding and specialist plant and machinery. Choose subcontractors who have been recommended and those who have worked together before. This makes coordination a little easier and there is less likely to be conflict. You will need to visit the site quite regularly to ensure one trade has finished before sending in another or to even to check that a subcontractor has turned up!

Tenders from a List of Contractors

This is the traditional route for procurement, whereby a list of suitable contractors is drawn up and tenders invited from them. This is the method the professionals use as it gives a competitive price for the whole of the works. The tenders are based on specifications and drawings and normally include the specialist subcontractor packages.

Preferred Contractor

This method relies on the quotation submitted by a preferred contractor, or one who has been recommended and who can demonstrate successful and satisfactory completion of similar work. This route can give excellent results, although there is no certainty that the price given is competitive unless a professional has been used. This method can often get you on site faster. Avoid using a friend if you can as it can lead to losing the friendship permanently if things go wrong!

There are, of course, hybrids of the methods discussed above and your conversion may call for a different approach. Architects and surveyors will be able to advise on the most suitable method.

CHOOSING A CONTRACTOR

Recommendation is the best method, whether it is based on work by a contractor you have seen and liked or heard about from friends or professionals. Most likely you will be a novice at building, and as with all such things you will be on a steep learning curve. There are many pitfalls in choosing a contractor, as evidenced by press and television reports of the havoc caused by 'cowboy' builders. How do you spot the difference between bona fide contractors and their less than reputable colleagues and ensure that you hire a good one?

Use of a Professional

Building professionals are normally the best source of advice and if you intend using one it is better to let them make recommendations as to suitable contractors and subcontractors.

Recommendation

Even if a contractor has been highly recommended you should always visit samples of their work and talk to their clients. Ask questions such as:

- Was the work completed on time?
- Was the contractor organized and worked to an agreed programme?
- Did the contractor ask for money up front? (A sure sign of an inexperienced or 'cowboy' builder.)
- Is the work guaranteed?
- Did the contractor employ good subcontractors? Did they turn up on time?
- Were there any defects that had to be put right? If so, have they been remedied satisfactorily?
- Were there any extra costs that seemed excessive?
- Did the contractor follow the specifications and drawings?

Ask Around

Local tradesmen will give their opinions, but it is the local building inspector who is most likely to know who is good or bad. Whilst he cannot condemn a builder outright, he will be able to give pointers.

Yellow Pages

This is the last resort and is pretty much pot luck. However, architects have been known to use this method. If you need to go down this road, then shortlist suitable contractors and invite them to interview. Ask them what conversion work they have done and make arrangements to visit examples. Enquire about insurances and public liability cover.

OBTAINING A QUOTATION

You may already have a rough estimate or have been given an indication of cost by your architect. However, it is only when the contractor has actually priced the specification and drawings and made an offer that you have any certainty of what the conversion works are going to cost. The most common method of obtaining a quote is by competitive tendering. This is where a number of contractors submit sealed bids based on the specifications and drawings. The bids are normally submitted in writing and returned on a preset day and opened by the client or the client's architect.

These bids constitute offers to do the work for a fixed sum, by an agreed date, and should remain open for acceptance for at least a month. This is where market forces take a hand; it is the moment of truth, whereby you may be pleasantly surprised if the tenders have come in below estimate or in despair if they have come in well above. In the latter case, apart from abandoning the project, there are various options that can be considered:

- **Negotiate with the lowest tenderer** You can discuss with the contractor whether there are any items that could be reduced in cost. This is an area where you will need the advice of a quantity surveyor or architect who has experience in negotiation.
- **Omit sections of the work** If you can take out non-essential sections, then this can produce real cost savings. You could carry out these sections later when you have more money.
- **Reduce the specification of the works** You may have to reduce the quality of some of the finishes and make do with cheaper alternatives. This will not produce great cost savings, but

may be the difference that enables the project to proceed.

- **Obtain extra finance** Whilst this is may be an option, it may not be palatable to you or acceptable by your financial backer.

You should, of course, check the arithmetic of the lowest tender before embarking on any further action, as it is quite common for a contactor to make errors. However, under tendering conditions, he can either stand by the error and let his tender remain for consideration, or if the error means that he has seriously underpriced the works, then he has the option to withdraw from the bidding.

When judging the tenders, it may not always be the lowest bid that is the most acceptable. For example, if the next lowest bid is from a very reputable firm and one that is noted for the quality of its work and ability to finish on time, it should also be considered, especially if the price difference is not too great.

CONTRACTS

The successful contractor should be contacted as soon as possible, but you should also not forget to inform the unsuccessful bidders of the result of the tender process. The contractor will want to make preliminary arrangements, such as ordering materials and appointing subcontractors, so you may be required to issue a letter of appointment. This is where care is needed and it is preferable to use professional advice. The tender bid constitutes an offer and any form of written acceptance will form a simple but binding contract. This may be all that is strictly necessary, but should any dispute arise between you and the contractor and you have cause to go to litigation, then this document will be used as the basis of any settlement.

You may have heard about 'letters of intent', which are when a client writes to the contractor informing him that he intends to place an order or enter into a contract with him. Unless professionals word these letters, they are to be avoided as you have unwittingly entered into a binding contract.

The best procedure is to have a suitable contract drawn up prior to the contractor's appointment.

There are numerous forms available, but the ones most commonly used are those produced by the Joint Contracts Tribunal (JCT), an independent body set up by various construction bodies, which includes representatives from consulting engineers, builders and specialist contractors, architects, surveyors and representatives from local government and the British Property Federation. In Scotland the equivalent body is the Scottish Building Contract Committee.

There are two forms of JCT contract that are best suited for conversion works:

- *Agreement for Minor Building Works* (in Scotland, *Scottish Minor Works Contract – without quantities*).
- *Building Contract for a home owner/occupier,* or the newer *Building Contract for a home owner/occupier who has appointed a consultant,* plus the associated *Consultancy Agreement* (*not for use in Scotland*).

These are contracts meant for projects costing between £20,000 and £100,000, but they are commonly used for larger schemes that are not too complex. For the bigger, more complicated schemes involving many subcontractors, the JCT *Intermediate Form of Contract (IFC98)* is more suitable, though not often appropriate for conversion projects.

The *Agreement for Minor Building Works* has been around since 1998 and was last revised in 2002. It is the one most commonly used by architects, being easily adapted to suit most situations and quite straightforward to administer. However, the Agreement is only intended for use where the client/customer has appointed a professional consultant to advise and administer its terms.

The Agreement is thirty pages long and divided into four sections including a guidance note, which is generally set out as below:

A. **Recitals** These contain a brief description of the proposed work and who will administer the contract, whether a quantity surveyor (QS) is to

OPPOSITE: Front page of Agreement for Minor Building Works 1998. (© The Joint Contracts Tribunal Ltd 2001)

JCT

Agreement for Minor Building Works

This Agreement is only intended for use where the Client has engaged a professional consultant to advise on and to administer its terms.

This Agreement

is made the ___*9th*___ day of ___*August*___ 19 *99*

BETWEEN ___*Peace Haven Developments Plc*___

of ___*Bury Port, Marshville*___

(hereinafter called 'the Employer') of the one part

AND ___*Weathervain Builders*___

of (or whose registered office is at) ___*Cheapside Thawbridge*___

(hereinafter called 'the Contractor') of the other part.

MW 98

be appointed, and a list of the documents to be attached to the contract, such as drawings and specification. There is a statement on whether or not the CDM (Construction (Design and Management)) Regulations apply.

B. **Articles** This section sets out the contractor's obligations, contract sum and names of the architect or contract administrator (CA), the planning supervisor, the contractor and details of dispute resolution, that is, adjudication, arbitration or legal proceedings.

C. **Conditions** This section is divided up into eight headings which generally deal with:

1. **Intentions of the Parties to the Contract** The contractor's obligations, the architects or CA's duties and duties under the CDM regulations.

2. **Commencement and Completion Date** Start and completion, extensions of time, damages for non-completion and defects liability period.

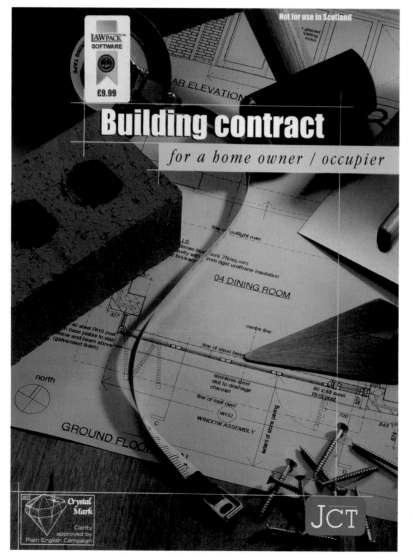

Front cover of Building Contract for a home owner/occupier.
(© The Joint Contracts Tribunal Ltd 2001)

3. **Control of the Works** Assignment and subletting of the works by the contractor, the architect's or CA's instructions, variations to the contract and treatment of provisional sums (PS).

4. **Payments** Progress stages and retention, including notices of amounts to be paid and deductions to be made. The issue of Certificates for payment including interim, penultimate and final certificates.

5. **Statutory Obligations** Payment of statutory charges and VAT; also the Employer's obligations, for example appointment of planning

Front cover of Consultancy Agreement for a home owner/occupier appointing a consultant to provide building consultancy services. (© The Joint Contracts Tribunal Ltd 2001)

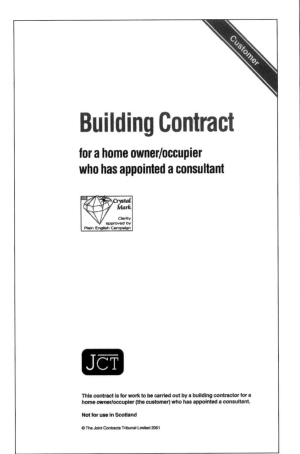

Front cover of Building Contract for a home owner/occupier who has appointed a consultant. (© The Joint Contracts Tribunal Ltd 2001)

supervisor if required and production of the Health & Safety File if applicable (*see* Chapter 4).

6. **Injury, Damage and Insurance.**

7. **Determination** Of the contract by either the employer or the contractor. (Bringing the contract to an end.)

8. **Settlement of Disputes** By adjudication, arbitration or legal proceedings.

D. **Supplemental Conditions** Contains further references to payments of statutory fees, tax changes, VAT and dispute resolution.

	Contract with a Consultant	Without a Consultant
Part 1.	**The Arrangements for the Work** **A.** **The work to be done:** Brief description of the works, including relevant documents and quotations.	
	B. **Planning permission, building regulations and party walls:** States that applications have been made or are to be made by the consultant and the duty of contractor not to commence works on site without planning permission.	Applications are to be made by either the contractor or customer.
	C. **Using facilities on the premises:** Facilities to be allowed free of charge to the contractor are detailed.	
	D. **Price:** The price for the work including VAT is recorded and takes into account unexpected problems that could not be foreseen.	The costs for making applications to be reimbursed to the contractor.
	E **Payment:** Conditions for payment by either lump sum or stages, including provisions for retention.	
	F. **The working period:** The start and finish dates for the work (or number of weeks).	
	G. **Product guarantees:** Contractor to pass any guarantees on to employer.	
	H. **Insurance:** The customer is to inform his or her insurers prior to commencement of the works at the insured premises. The contractor is required to have an 'All Risks' policy to cover the work and materials.	
	I. **Working hours:** To be stated.	
	J. **Occupation and security of the premises:** The customer is to state whether or not the premises will be occupied and the contractor is thus obliged to take any necessary precautions.	
	K. **Disputes:** The procedures for dispute resolution are outlined.	
Part 2.	**The Conditions** **1.** **Contractor's responsibilities:** The obligations of carrying out the work are stated and in particular the contractor is to proceed carefully, competently, work to time and to the drawings and specifications and to the instructions of the consultant.	Omission of reference to instructions of the consultant.
	2. **Customer's responsibilities:** The customer is to provide access and not obstruct the contractor.	

	Contract with a Consultant	Without a Consultant
3.	**The consultant's role:** The consultant is to act for customer, issue instructions and extend timescales if necessary. He will issue a certificate when the work has been completed and one when all the faults, which have occurred during the contract, have been remedied.	Clause omitted.
4.	**Health and safety:** The contractor will take steps to prevent or minimize risks to health and safety to the customer and others using the premises. The customer will take notice of any health and safety warnings given by the contractor and not allow anyone to visit the premises during the construction.	
5.	**Changing the work details:** The consultant alone can change the details of the work on behalf of the customer. If these changes increase the amount of work, the contractor can quote for the extras. If they reduce the amount then the price should be adjusted to show a saving.	The customer alone can change the details of the work.
6.	**Extending the work period:** The consultant can extend the period of the contract if any changes have increased the amount of work or for occurrences beyond the control of the contractor. The contractor can claim additional costs caused by the customer or consultant.	The customer can extend the working period.
7.	**Certifying the finished work:** A final certificate is issued at the completion of all the work.	Clause omitted.
8.	**Payment:** Sets out conditions for making stage payments. The contractor's invoice to be 95% of payment certified (to take into account retention) and if the consultant is satisfied the customer is to pay within fourteen days after receipt. The retention is released when the consultant confirming all defects have been remedied issues the final certificate.	The customer is to be satisfied that the contractor's interim invoices are correct and that all defects have been remedied at final payment.
9.	**Contractor's continuing responsibility:** The contractor will remain responsible for six years for any faults caused by him, other than for fair wear and tear during this period.	
10.	**Bringing the contract to an end:** If the contractor is in breach for not regularly carrying out the work or is incompetent etc., and after written warning does not rectify the situation then the contract can be ended after due notice. If the customer does not pay amounts that have been certified and due or prevents the contractor from carrying out the work etc., and after written warning does not rectify the situation,	Reference to consultant omitted.

continued on page 134

continued from page 133

	Contract with a Consultant	Without a Consultant
	then the contract is ended after due notice. Failure by the consultant to perform his duties properly can also bring the contract to an end. **11. Insolvency:** If either the contractor or customer becomes insolvent then the contract can come to an end unless insolvency arrangements are made to allow it to proceed. If the contractor becomes insolvent the customer will only pay what is due to him until another contractor has completed the works. **12. Other rights and remedies:** The contractor and the customer can make cost and expense claims against each other and take any legal remedies. **13. Law of contract:** The laws of England and Wales apply.	

The much shorter and simpler *Building Contract for a home owner/occupier* is intended for householders who plan to deal directly with a builder for improvements, extensions and repairs. It is in general unsuitable for larger projects and where a consultant is likely to be appointed. The contract is in two parts: Part 1, the Arrangements for the work, is set out in a carbonized pad of eight pages (four yellow top copies and four pink duplicates) and Part 2, the Conditions, runs to four pages.

If the project is likely to be a bit larger and you intend to appoint a consultant, then the *Building Contract for a home owner/occupier who has appointed a consultant* is more suitable. It is almost identical to the contract above and again runs to eight pages (four pages for the Arrangement for the work and four for the Conditions).

The main difference is that it comes with a *Consultancy Agreement* and some of the clauses within the contract have been modified to take into account the consultant's role. Both contracts set out in plain English what the basic conditions of the contract are and, if appointed, the services of the consultant. The parties to these building contracts are the customer and the contractor *only*, and never the consultant. The contract using a consultant is in time likely to be used in preference to the *Minor Works Contract*

(*MW98*), as it is far easier to understand and makes it clear what the consultant should be doing.

The first page of the contract records the name and address of the customer and the address where the work will be done. The contractor's name and address is recorded along with that of the consultant if one is to be appointed. The contracts are divided into two parts generally as follows and can be compared as shown in the chart.

The *Consultancy Agreement* has a similar format to the contract and the first page again records the name and address of the customer and the location for the works. The consultant's name and address are recorded, and also his profession. These are the only parties to the agreement, and not the contractor.

If more than one consultant is appointed, then you will need separate agreements with each of them. There is no reason why the Consultancy Agreement cannot be used in conjunction with the *Minor Works Contract* (*MW98*) or with any other contract if desired or even on its own.

The agreement is divided into two parts:

Part 1. The Consultant's Services

A. **The Services** The consultant provides a whole range of services before building work commences and during operations on site. These are all detailed in the agreement and can be added or omitted as necessary.

B. **Consultant's Fees** The total fee expected is recorded and the amounts to be paid at stage intervals are also written down. The hourly rate is stated for any works done on an hourly basis. If any changes are made to the works then the consultant's fees can be increased or reduced accordingly.

C. **Insurance** The consultant shall state the minimum amount of PII held and on request provide the customer with evidence of cover.

D. **Disputes** The parties to the agreement can start court proceedings to settle disputes or have them decided by an adjudicator.

Part 2. The Conditions

1. **Consultant's Responsibilities** The consultant will act as the customer's representative and carry out services with due regard to law and act with reasonable care, skill and attention. The consultant will issue certificates and give instructions, which are to be fair to both the customer and the contractor. The consultant shall not subcontract any of his services without the customer's permission.

2. **Customer's Responsibilities** The customer must reveal any relevant information to allow the consultant to carry out his services. The customer should consider the consultant's advice and allow only the consultant to deal with the contractor and not interfere with any instruction given or certificates issued.

3. **Changing the Services** The customer can change the services required of the consultant. If this results in an increase in the service to be provided, then the consultant is entitled to an extra fee, and conversely if it results in a reduction of service then his fee should be reduced accordingly.

4. **Paying the Consultant's Fee** The customer is to pay for the services provided by the consultant at the completion of each stage. The consultant's

invoice is to be paid no later than fourteen days from the date of issue.

5. **Consultant's Continuing Responsibility** This is to be six years after the provision of the services.

6. **Copyright** The consultant will hold the copyright to any documents produced for the works, but the customer and contractor will be allowed copies for future works or maintenance to the premises.

7. **Bringing This Agreement to an End** Prior to signing the building contract, and after seven days' written notice, either party can end this agreement. If after signing the building contract either party is in breach of the agreement, then after seven days' written notice this agreement can be ended. The agreement can be ended if either party becomes insolvent.

8. **Other Rights and Remedies** Either party can claim costs and expenses resulting from not abiding by this agreement and can take any legal remedies.

9. **Law of the Agreement** The laws of England and Wales apply.

An alternative to this is to have a contract prepared online by filling out a simple questionnaire. Some legal firms provide such a service for about £30. These are tailored building contracts for use by builders and homeowners/occupiers in England and Wales and follow a similar format to the JCT forms outlined above.

Useful Information and Contacts

Specification:
- National Building Specification.
  Tel. 0845 456 9594 – *www.theNBS.com*

Contracts:
- RIBA Bookshops. Tel. 020 7256 7222 – *www.ribabookshops.com*
- Construction Industry Publications Ltd. Tel. 0870 878 440 – *www.cip-books.com*
- Joints Contract Tribunal. – *www.jctltd.co.uk*

CHAPTER 8

Project Planning, Administration and Operations on Site

PROJECT PLANNING

Management

The objective of good project management is summed up by the phrase 'Getting the right building at the right price at the right time'. Project management consists of both taking an overview and, where necessary, micro-managing. It is not to be confused with managing just the building work itself. Project management is one of the most difficult aspects of any project. It is especially difficult for those who have never been involved in a building project before.

Any project is a combination of three elements – time, cost and quality – which have to be managed effectively:

- **Time** This is the programme from inception to the completion of the works and finally occupying the premises.
- **Cost** This includes every cost from day one, when you have chosen your building, to moving in. It can also be the original budget, the current cost or the forecast.
- **Quality** This refers to suitability for purpose and specification of finishes and materials.

At the outset of a project there will be considerations of how long the project will take, how much is it likely to cost and what quality of building will be achieved. You will arrive initially at a balance of time against cost against quality. This is the model or plan by which all later decisions and events are tested. If one of the elements is changed, for example the

building work costs more than the budget in the early stages, overall costs are likely to increase, but the specification could be reduced to compensate and the project may still keep within budget. Or the work may take longer, leading to the addition of temporary accommodation costs and finance charges may increase. Things will keep changing and will need managing to mitigate any damaging effects to the project.

The project manager, whether it is yourself or a professional employed by you, needs to work to some form of checklist. This needs to contain all the stages of the process and every major item you can think of, in roughly the order they are likely to occur and who will be responsible for them. This list avoids confusion about who is doing what and gives a target date by which to get things done. It must be continually updated. Regular meetings with the architect or consultant should be held to review the items on the list and to monitor their progress. The example checklist presented here can be expanded to include priorities and other items you may wish to monitor.

Time (Programming)

Time can be the biggest enemy, as everything appears to take twice as long as planned. It is therefore extremely important to set a realistic programme at the outset. It is no use just plucking a number from thin air. You need to schedule each work stage and then set a time period for each one. You should also analyse the schedule to determine which item of work is on a critical path, that is, which item is dependent on the previous and which items are

Project Planning Checklist

Project Stage	Work to be Undertaken	Due Date Complete	Percentage	Status	Action By
1. Feasibility	Check planning situation	1 Aug	100%	Done	Client
	Arrange finance in principle	5 Aug	100%	Done	Client
	Make offer subject to planning approval/survey	10 Aug	100%	Accepted	Client
	Arrange survey	25 Aug	100%	Done	Client/ surveyor
2. Outline proposals	Appoint architect or consultant	1 Sep	100%	Done	Client
	Prepare brief	5 Sep	100%	Done	Client/ architect
	Prepare sketch plans and estimates	19 Sep	100%	Done	Architect
3. Scheme design	Prepare outline programme	25 Sep	100%	Dependent on planning approval	Architect
	Finalize finance	30 Sep	50%	In progress	Client
	Consult with planners, local authorities and statutory undertakers		50%	In progress	Architect
	Prepare outline proposals for planning			Done	Architect
	Submit proposals to Planning Authority	17 Oct	100%	Done	Architect
	On receipt of planning approval finalize purchase	12 Dec	25%		Client
4. Detailed design	Prepare detailed drawings	17 Nov	40%		Architect
	Prepare and submit applications for approval under Building Regulations	17 Nov	0%		Architect
	Appoint other consultants as required		25%		Client/ architect
5. Production information	Prepare production (working) drawings	18 Dec	0%		Architect
	Prepare specification (and information for B of Q)	2 Jan	0%		Architect
	Coordinate other consultants information		0%		Architect

continued on page 138

continued from page 137

Project Stage	Work to be Undertaken	Due Date Complete	Percentage	Status	Action By
6. Tender action	Prepare list of contractors for tender		0%		Client/ architect
	Invite tenders	23 Jan	0%		Architect
	Report on tenders received	30 Jan	0%		Architect
7. Project planning	Prepare building contract	30 Jan	0%		Architect
	Arrange for any subcontract to be instructed		0%		Architect
	Appoint contractor	30 Jan	0%		Client/ architect
8. Operations on Site	Start on site	2 Feb	0%		Client/ architect
	Completion of internal works	14 May	0%		Architect
	Move in	21 May	0%		Client
	Completion of external works	27 May	0%		Client

Task Name	Start	Fini
Prepare & agree brief	Mon 01/09/03	Fri 0!
Prepare sketch plans & estimate	Mon 08/09/03	Fri 1!
Prepare & submit proposals for Planning	Mon 22/09/03	Fri 1!
Planning Application consideration	Mon 20/10/03	Fri 1!
Prepare detailed drawings and submit for Building Regs	Mon 20/10/03	Mon 1!
Building Regs approval period	Tue 18/11/03	Tue 3(
Prepare production (working)drawings	Tue 18/11/03	Thu 1!
Prepare specification	Fri 19/12/03	Fri 0!
Tender period	Mon 05/01/04	Fri 2!
Tender report & prepare contracts	Mon 26/01/04	Fri 3(
Building contract period (internal works)	Mon 02/02/04	Fri 1!
Building contract (external works)	Tue 04/05/04	Thu 2!
Move in	Mon 17/05/04	Fri 2!

A simple bar chart program showing each of the main tasks that make up the project. The arrows link the tasks by start and completion, with the solid bars showing the progress to date.
(Barrie Davies)

independent and can run concurrently with the others. There are computer packages that will help with this – a typical programme is Microsoft Project®, which is simple and quite straightforward to use. The illustration shown here is of a relatively simple project, and does not take into account the months prior to appointing the architect.

You will note that each activity bar on the programme is linked to one or more of the others. This denotes a linkage and that one activity must finish before the other begins, for example the planning and Building Regulations consideration periods must be completed before work starts on site. You will also note that within some of the activity bars there is a thick solid line, which indicates progress achieved on that activity.

Costs

You will have previously prepared a budget of all the costs likely to be incurred (*see* Chapter 3). The property will have been purchased, drawings prepared and the necessary approvals obtained. Quotations and tenders for the building works will have been gathered in. In addition, you should have been comparing budget costs with actual costs and keeping a constant record. A typical expenditure recording log is shown here; it is based on a normal computer spreadsheet, which updates automatically as entries are made.

Based on orders placed and on payments made, you can prepare an *estimated actual* or forecast, which is the sum of all the *estimated* and *actual* costs to date. This is, with the information available to date, what the project is likely to cost and is a very useful tool for managing and reviewing current and future or even proposed additional expenditure.

Changes in specification, finishes and size have proportional effects on cost. Reducing the quality of specified items and finishes can lead to cost savings, as does omitting sections of the work. However, it is quite a problem to deal with contractors over savings, as you never seem to get back as much as you would

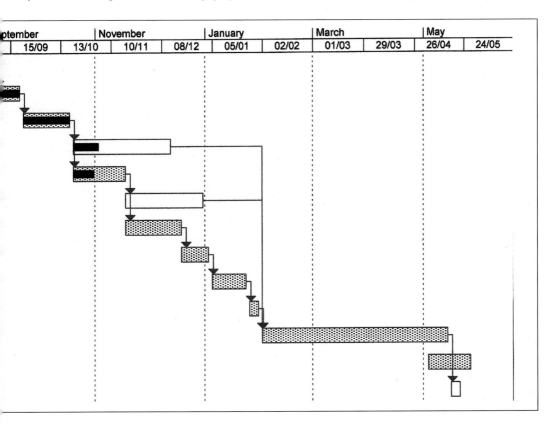

Expenditure Log	A Budget	B Supplier	C Order value	D Variation: Budget/Order (Column A-C)	E Payment 1	F Payment 2	G Payment 3	H Payment 4	I Payment 5	J Paid to date (Columns E,F,G,H & I)	K Balance to Pay (Column C-J)	L Estimated Actual
1. Purchase cost	£75,000	Mr & Mrs A Vendor	£75,000	£0	£7,500	£67,500				£75,000	£0	£75,000
2. Building works												
Main Contractor	£85,000	Convert Barnswell Ltd	£80,000	£5,000	£10,000	£16,000	£18,000	£25,000		£69,000	£11,000	£85,000
Electrical	£18,000	H E Sparks & Co	£20,000	-£2,000	£2,500	£6,000	£8,000			£16,500	£3,500	£21,000
Heating	£10,000	B Warmpots & Co	£10,000	£0	£1,000	£5,000	£2,500			£8,500	£1,500	£10,000
Own labour and materials	£6,000		£5,500	£500	£1,250	£2,000	£1,000	£500		£6,250	-£750	£7,000
External works (Budget £125,000)	£6,000	Overgreens Ltd	£6,000	£0	£3,000	£2,000	£1,000			£5,000	£1,000	£6,000
3. Legal fees	£5,000	Leagle & Beagle	£5,200	-£200	£2,500	£2,700				£5,200	£0	£5,200
4. Stamp duty	£150	Inland Revenue	£150	£0	£150					£150	£0	£150
5. Valuation & arrangement fees	£400	N Cash & Co	£350	£50	£350					£350	£0	£350
6. Site survey fees	£1,000	Theo Dolite Ptrs	£1,100	-£100	£1,100					£1,100	£0	£1,100
7. Design fees	£12,500	C Wren & Partners	£12,500	£0	£5,000	£1,500	£1,200			£7,700	£4,800	£12,500
8. Structural engineers fees	£500	T Telford & Son	£500	£0	£250	£250				£500	£0	£500
9. Planning application fees	£220	SUDC	£220	£0	£220					£220	£0	£195
10. Building Regulation fees	£750	SUDC	£750	£0	£398					£398	£352	£398
11. Insurance premiums	£2,000	C Overall Brokers	£1,850	£150	£1,250	£600				£1,850	£0	£1,850
12. Service connection charges	£2,500	Watergen	£3,000	-£500	£1,200	£1,800				£3,000	£0	£3,000
13. Alternative accommodation	£2,500	Caravan on site	£2,100	£400	£2,100					£2,100	£0	£2,100
14. Removal costs	£1,000	TBA		£1,000						£0	£0	£1,000
Total	£228,520		£224,220	£4,300						£202,818		£232,343
Unbudgeted Additional Expenditure												
15. Storage sheds	£0	Overgreens Ltd	£1,200	-£1,200	£1,200					£1,200	£0	£1,200
16. Boundary fencing and walling	£0	Overgreens Ltd	£2,500	-£2,500	£1,250	£1,250				£2,500	£0	£2,500
New Total	£228,520		£227,920	£600						£206,518		£236,043
										Increase over budget		3.29%

LEFT: *An example of an expenditure recording log. This can be as detailed or as simple as you require.* (Barrie Davies)

OPPOSITE: *An* Architect's Instruction *form, which can be used with the* Agreement for Minor Building Works 1998. *The* Contract Administrator's Instruction *form is similar.* (© RIBA Enterprises)

Issued by: address:	Ivor Barch Associates Prospects Drive, Thawbridge	**Architect's Instruction**

19

Employer: address:	Peace Haven Developments Plc Bury Port, Marshville

Job reference: IBA/98/16

Instruction no: 5

Contractor: address:	Weathervain Builders Cheapside, Thawbridge

Issue date: 24 September 1999

Sheet: 1   of   1

Works: situated at:	Renovations and alterations Marine Buildings, Thawbridge

Agreement
Contract dated: 9 August 1999

Under the terms of the above-mentioned Contract, I/we issue the following instructions:

	Office use: Approximate costs	
	£ omit	£ add
1. EXTRACT FAN, WC/2 Supply and fix 1 no. 'Loovent' as per specification ref. N10/30 to wall of 1st floor WC/2 ducted to the outside through the adjoining roof using roof cowl accessories.	–	500.00
2. FIRE COMPARTMENTATION IN ROOFSPACE Provide 2 no. one-hour fire-resistant partitions in roofspace over the original party wall positions comprising a stud framework and 2 no. layers 12.5mm Wondaboard screwed to each side and sealed in accordance with manufacturer's recommendations.	–	500.00
3. NEW CONCRETE CILLS TO BAYS Replace 3 no. cracked Bath Stone cills to window bays to ground floor main elevation. Use 3 no. precast concrete cills of dimensions to match existing stonework.	–	250.00

This instruction is issued under clauses 3.5 and 3.6 of the contract.

Note
There are likely to be health and safety implications for item
2 above. Information on any adjustments found necessary to
your Health and Safety Plan should be submitted to us and
direct to the Employer and the Planning Supervisor for
information.

To be signed by or for the issuer named above	Signed *Ivor Barch*	1,250.00

Amount of Contract Sum	£	83,389.00
± Approximate value of previous Instructions	£	5,300.00
Sub-total	£	88,689.00
± Approximate value of this Instruction	£	1,250.00
Approximate adjusted total	£	89,939.00

Distribution			
☐ Contractor	☐ Quantity Surveyor	☐ Clerk of Works	☐
☐ Employer	☐ Structural Engineer	☐ Planning Supervisor	☐
☐ Nominated Sub-Contractors	☐ M&E Consultant	☐	☐ File

F809   for JCT 98 / IFC 98 / MW 98   © RIBA Publications 1999

Certificate of

Progress Payment

MW 98

25

Issued by: address:	Ivor Barch Associates Prospects Drive, Thawbridge

Employer: address:	Peace Haven Developments Plc Bury Port, Marshville	Serial no:	**J**
		Job reference:	IBA/98/16
Contractor: address:	Weathervain Builders Cheapside, Thawbridge	Certificate no:	2
		Date of issue:	8 October 1999
Works: situated at:	Renovations and alterations Marine Buildings, Thawbridge	Final date for payment:	22 October 1999

Agreement dated: 9 August 1999

Original to Employer

*Delete as appropriate.

* This certificate of progress payment

~~* This penultimate certificate~~

is issued under the terms of the above-mentioned Agreement.

[1] Percentage is normally 5% except where practical completion has been achieved (2.5%) or where some other percentage has been agreed by the parties.

Value of work executed and of materials and goods on site	£	35,000.000
[1] *Less* retention of **5** %	£	1,750.000
Sub-total	£	33,250.000
Less total amounts previously certified	£	8,360.000
Net amount for payment	£	24,890.000

I/We hereby certify that the **amount of progress payment** due to the Contractor is (in words)

All amounts are exclusive of VAT.

Twenty Four Thousand Eight Hundred and Ninety Pounds.

To be signed by or for the issuer named above

Signed *Ivor Barch.*

[2] Relevant only if clause B1·1 of the Supplemental Conditions applies. Delete if not applicable.

[2] The Contractor has given notice that the rate of VAT chargeable on the supply of goods and services to which the Agreement relates is 17.5 %

[2] 17.5 % of the amount certified above	£	4,355.75
[2] Total of net amount and VAT amount (for information)	£	29,245.75

This is not a Tax Invoice.

F851C for MW 98

© RIBA Publications 1999

have anticipated. This seems especially true when the project is on site, when you appear to receive less back than if the omission was made at tender stage. Omissions, whilst offering the greatest potential for savings, often have hidden 'add backs', in that making an omission can lead to having to do something else instead, which will have cost implications and thus reduce the initial saving.

Quality

The contract documents spell out clearly what is to be built, installed and fitted. Each element used in the building would have been specified by the consultant as to supplier, manufacturer, type, size, colour, weight and so on. It is common for contractors to offer alternatives to those specified, especially if the original item is unavailable. Sometimes they are equivalents, but often they are of inferior quality. You have to be continually on your guard when agreeing to change specified items. It is always good practice to know exactly what has been specified and for what purpose before you make any decisions.

For the inexperienced, the quality of workmanship is a minefield. Do you really know how things should be done properly? If you do not and you have not appointed a professional, then this is the prime area where some contractors may attempt to get away with less than adequate build quality and cut corners (see 'Site Supervision' below).

CONTRACT ADMINISTRATION

Instructions

You have instructed the contractor to proceed, or your consultant has done so on your behalf. However, before work starts it is essential to be clear regarding everyone's responsibilities. If an architect has been appointed, then he accepts your instructions and puts them into a formal written instruction (*Architect's Instruction* or *Contract Administrator's Instruction*) to the contractor. The better contractors

OPPOSITE: The certificate of Progress Payment. *These certificates maintain a running total of the contract costs.* (© RIBA Enterprises)

are used to working with architects and know at their peril that they should not accept instructions directly from the client for fear of not being paid. A client's instruction has no validity unless confirmed in writing by the architect.

If you are dealing directly with the contractor, without an architect, then all instructions should be recorded and given to the contract's manager, never the workmen. A simple way of doing this is to obtain from a stationer a duplicate book with numbered pages and write down the instruction and date it, tear off the top copy and hand it to the contractor. You then have the bound duplicates in number and date sequence to which you can refer. With only verbal instructions and without written evidence it is very difficult to settle extras at the end of the contract.

Payments

If a consultant is appointed, then payments are made in the form of *Progress Payment Certificates*, which are issued following each application for payment made by the contractor. These are usually monthly, and from the date of issue of the certificate you are bound by the contract to pay the contractor within fourteen days the amount certified by the consultant as being due. Certificates represent the value of work completed to date and materials on site. However, only 95 per cent of the value is paid to the contractor, with the remaining 5 per cent kept as retention.

The purpose of a retention is to cover making good any defects that may arise and provide the employer with security for the contractor's performance, obligations and quality of the work. Each subsequent certificate attracts 5 per cent retention, and the accumulated fund, which should be held in a separate bank account, is kept until the work is complete.

At completion, a penultimate certificate is issued, releasing the total value of the completed works to the contractor minus the retention, which is 5 per cent under the *Building Contract for a home owner/ occupier* and 2½ per cent under the *Agreement for Minor Building Works*. This retention is ultimately released under a final certificate after a period of three months under the *Homeowners Building Contract for a home owner/occupier* and six months under the *Agreement for Minor Building Works*. This length of time is referred to as the 'defects liability period' (*see below* 'Contract Completion' and 'Defects Liability Period').

Expect paying a contractor without the services of a consultant to be fraught with difficulties. Overpayment is a common problem, as it can be difficult for the inexperienced to judge that a contractor is really due what he is claiming. Or you may have paid too much in advance and not have sufficient left for another contractor to complete the works should the original contractor cease trading.

One way to avoid problems while still being fair to the contractor is to agree monthly stage payments of a set amount. The amount would be equal to the contract sum divided by the number of months for which the contract is intended to run. You would need to monitor carefully that progress on site is matching the agreed programme. If the work goes behind or regular progress is not being maintained, and you continue to make stage payments, then you will certainly end up overpaying. If any extras to the contract have been carried out then the cost of these should be added to the monthly payments.

Extensions of Time

There is provision in the contract for an 'extension of time', that is, extending the working period and thus the length of the contract. The contractor can ask for the contract period to be increased due to any changes, which may have increased the amount of work, or for circumstances beyond his control, for example exceptionally inclement weather or late deliveries.

The consultant will extend the period by a number of days or weeks if he agrees with the contractor, but will base the period on the actual delay and not necessarily the contractor's claim. The consultant can issue a *Notification of an Extension of Time*, which will state the new date for completion. This results in the contractor being able to claim additional costs for any delay or disruption due to any changes in instructions caused by either the client or the consultant. He has to pay his men or not whether they are working and will want you to foot the bill!

If you are tackling the project yourself then you will need to realize that any changes of mind can lead

to delays and the risk of the contractor asking for further remuneration in addition to the cost of the extra work. You will have to judge whether or not these claims are justified – this is the area that causes the most disputes even when you have employed a consultant.

Extras

Extras are normally the result of changes to the specification or they arise from additional work. It is common for the novice client to think of extras as being already included and he or she will often see no reason to pay more. After all, this is what was wanted in the first place and the contractor should have known this all along!

The issue of extras to the contract and their value is a problem that can escalate very quickly. Try always to obtain firm quotations in writing for any extra work prior to agreeing to proceed. Keep a record of extras as they occur, along with the cost, or, if not available, an approximation. This, in addition to the record of instructions given, will greatly assist you in settling the final account.

Contractors can often make more profit on extras than on the original contract, so this is therefore an area in which to be wary. To say that a contractor can charge what he likes for extras is perhaps unfair, but he will no longer be under tender conditions and may be less competitive.

Final Account

As its name suggests, this is the final bill for the works. For some, this bill can come as a bit of a shock, especially if records have not been maintained and the client is living in blissful ignorance as to the cost of changes and extras.

The final accounts are set out in a prescribed manner, with the contract sum at the top and the omissions and additions, whether with an AI

OPPOSITE: The form for Notification of an Extension of Time. *It indicates a new date for completion of the contract and gives the reason for the extension.* (© RIBA Enterprises)

Notification of an

Extension of Time

2:

MW 98

Issued by:	Ivor Barch Associates
address:	Prospects Drive, Thawbridge

Employer:	Peace Haven Developments Plc	
address:	Bury Port, Marshville	
		Job reference: IBA/98/16

Contractor:	Weathervain Builders	Notification no: 1
address:	Cheapside, Thawbridge	
		Issue date: 28 September 1999

Works:	Renovations and alterations
situated at:	Marine Buildings, Thawbridge

Agreement dated: 9 August 1999

Under the terms of the above-mentioned Agreement,

I/we hereby give notice that the time for completion of the Works

is extended beyond the date for completion stated in the Agreement or any later date previously fixed so as to expire on

17 December   20 1999

For reasons of additional work as described
in AI No. 5 dated 24 September 1999.

To be signed by or for the issuer named above   Signed *Ivor Barch*

Distribution				
	☐ Employer	☐ Structural Engineer	☐ Planning Supervisor	☐
	☐ Contractor	☐ M&E Consultant	☐	☐
	☐ Quantity Surveyor	☐ Clerk of Works	☐	☐ File

F855C   for MW 98   © RIBA Publications 1999

(Architect's Instruction) or not, balanced out to give either a figure to add to the contract sum or one to be subtracted from it. This gives a revised contract sum.

The final account also shows what has been paid to date and the balance owing. A typical final account is shown here.

Final Account			
Final Account for Conversion of Barn at Lower Meadow			
Contractor: Convert Barnswell Ltd Client: Mr & Mrs B Goodenough Consultant: C. Wren & Partners Date:			
	£ Omissions	£ Additions	£
1 **Contract Sum**			80,000.00
2 **Omit Provisional Sums**			
Kitchen units	4,000.00		
Sanitary fittings	2,000.00		
Repairs (unspecified)	1,000.00		
3 **Add**			
Supply kitchen units		4,500.00	
Supply sanitary fittings		1,800.00	
Repairs (unspecified)		2,000.00	
Fitted cupboards		500.00	
Install lintel		250.00	
Demolition of outbuilding and cart away		350.00	
Temp. services to caravan		300.00	
Extra drainage gullies		400.00	
Increase size of patio		1,200.00	
Upgrade rainwater goods		350.00	
Holes for heating contractor		350.00	
Sum totals	7,000.00	12,000.00	
Additions – omissions			5,000.00
New contract sum			**85,000.00**
Paid to date			–69,000.00
Balance to pay			16,000.00

The consultant will normally receive a draft of the final account from the contractor for him to check. If everything is in order then a final certificate is issued for payment. If you are managing the work yourself, you will receive the final account and will need to check it carefully. Your record of instructions and extras will come in handy and will provide a background, especially to the additions. Do not be afraid to question any item and ask for back-up papers or original invoices. Sometimes you can negotiate the price of individual items and suggest a reduction if you think the contractor is being unfair.

OPERATIONS ON SITE

Sequence of Operations

It is important to understand the sequence of operations on site. With a new build, the sequence is relatively straightforward, following a tried and tested routine. With conversions, every project is a 'one off'. Because you already have a building, albeit in a poor state, you have to consider the priorities and analyse what work can be carried out initially. Your first objective may be to get the building wind and watertight, especially if stage payments are to be achieved (*see* Chapter 3). The likely things to do first are to carry out demolitions, excavate for foundations and drainage and make structural repairs.

If the roof timbers are reasonably sound, then you could concentrate on the roof. The other area that could proceed is making good old walls, building new ones, making any new openings and installing windows. In other words, you would be concentrating on the external envelope and groundworks.

Then would come the interior works such as forming new floors, stairways, erection of stud partitions and the first-fix installation of services.

Next comes the finishing trades, with the plasterer then the services contractor doing the second fix, and finally the decorator and floor layer. The contractor will be used to preparing programmes and scheduling subcontractors' work within them; if this is acceptable, then this is the best course of action.

The shell being made wind and watertight. (Montresor Partnership)

Forming structural openings. (Montresor Partnership)

Site Supervision

The contractor and subcontractors have arrived and commenced work. If you are employing a main contractor, he will carry out all the site supervision and coordination for you. If you are employing trade contractors, then you or the consultant will have to coordinate their work and how one will dovetail with the other. Site supervision should not be confused with telling the contactors how to build; they should be experienced tradesmen who know their job, but they will need to be told what to build and when.

Site supervision is essentially a form of micro project management combined with the role of an inspector. Assuming that the drawings and specification are complete, the relevant form of contract is in place and the programme agreed, then all that is left to do is inspect the quality and progress of the works. Sounds simple, but it never is!

The first fixing of the electrical services. It is useful to have a photographic record of the services installations before they are covered with plaster. (Montresor Partnership)

On site, things invariably change or go wrong. Opening up the building can reveal hidden structural problems. Materials may not turn up on time, or may be delivered damaged or incorrect. Subcontractors may turn up late or not at all. You may change your mind about something, which means that works already carried out will have to be removed and new items ordered and installed. The programme itself can easily go behind if the contractor is dilatory, which could then lead to him making up time at the expense of quality. Expect the works on site to be constantly changing in response to external forces, some within control and others not.

Regular site inspections by the consultant or contract administrator help to iron out the problems as they occur and prevent minor problems escalating into major issues. Regular meetings with the contractor and the client also help to keep everyone informed as to what is going on.

If you are project managing yourself, you may find that problems become a personal issue, and it may be that you have the caused the situation in the first place. In addition, what you may think is unacceptable may in fact be good practice and in accordance with the specifications and drawings. By and large, it is better if you can employ a consultant who is experienced in site practice to look after your affairs objectively.

Site Meetings

Meetings are essential to review progress and coordinate any subcontractors. Architects and consultants will normally hold site meetings on a regular basis depending on the length of the contract. Minutes should be taken at each meeting and an agenda will be followed to ensure that all items are covered. Each meeting will be peculiar to the work involved, but common items discussed and recorded would include some or all of those shown in the example.

The importance of the meeting is to assist communication and to avoid confusion. In addition, everyone at the meeting will have been able to contribute and will know exactly what has been achieved and what problems still remain to be resolved. They will also be clear as to what is to be completed and who is responsible. Even without a consultant, it is a very straightforward matter to hold

---

Typical Agenda for Site Meeting

1. Those present (What capacity)
2. Health and safety (Accidents report)
3. Weather conditions and days lost (Freezing etc.)
4. Programme and progress (Progress against programme)
5. Contractor's report (Information required)
6. Subcontractors' reports
7. Instructions (Received and to be issued)
8. Payments (Costs to date and forecast)
9. Consents to be obtained (If any outstanding)
10. Date and time of next meeting

---

such meetings and if you are managing trade subcontractors it is vitally important.

Progress Photographs and Records

It is a good idea to take regular photographs during the works on site. A series of photographs should be taken from the same point at regular time intervals to show the progress of the works. If each photograph is dated then it can be used as evidence of lack of progress in any dispute. Photographs can remind you in the future of how things were built and where service runs are. They can show modifications that were not originally on the drawings or were too minor to be included on the 'as built' ones.

Where CDM Regulations apply (*see* Chapter 2), then it is the duty of the contractor to provide a *Health & Safety File* on completion. This needs to contain details of all equipment installed and details of any maintenance required, for example to glazing at high level. It must also contain a set of 'as built' drawings. While it is unlikely, that the Regulations will apply, you should insist that you are given all brochures and instructions on equipment installed and any drawings and information produced by specialist subcontractors or manufacturers. You should also insist on maintenance information on specialist finishes, flooring and so on.

If you have employed an architect you are entitled to set of 'as built' drawings, although as he is liable to be thinking about the next job and may forget, you

TOP LEFT: *Month one.*
(Montresor Partnership)

TOP RIGHT: *Month two.*
(Montresor Partnership)

LEFT: *Month three.*
(Montresor Partnership)

Month four.
(Montresor
Partnership)

OPPOSITE: *Certificate of*
Practical Completion.
(© RIBA Enterprises)

Certificate of

Practical Completion

MW 98

Issued by: Ivor Barch Associates
address: Prospects Drive, Thawbridge

Employer: Peace Haven Developments Plc
address: Bury Port, Marshville

Job reference: IBA/98/16

Contractor: Weathervain Builders
address: Cheapside, Thawbridge

Certificate no: 1

Issue date: 4 January 2000

Works: Renovations and alterations
situated at: Marine Buildings, Thawbridge

Agreement dated: 9 August 1999

Under the terms of the above-mentioned Agreement,

I/we hereby certify that in my/our opinion

practical completion of the Works has been achieved

*Delete if not
applicable

* and the Contractor has complied with the contractual requirements in
respect of information for the health and safety file

on   Friday 24 December   ~~26~~ 1999

To be signed by or for
the issuer named
above

Signed *Ivor Barch.*

Distribution	☐ Employer	☐ Structural Engineer	☐ Planning Supervisor	☐
	☐ Contractor	☐ M&E Consultant	☐	☐
	☐ Quantity Surveyor	☐ Clerk of Works	☐	☐ File

F853C   for MW 98

© RIBA Publications 1999

may need to remind him! These records are now becoming more important and with the advent of the 'Seller's Information Pack', they will prove invaluable.

Contract Completion

There are two distinct stages to the completion of any building contract. The first stage is known as practical completion, which is the acceptance by the consultant or yourself that the works have been completed and the building is ready for occupation. The second stage is known as final completion, and is usually three or six months afterwards (depending on the contract used).

At practical completion, you or the consultant must inspect the works and issue a schedule listing any works that are not complete and any defects found. A consultant normally will issue a *Certificate of Practical Completion*, which allows you to take possession and move in.

At the end of either the three or six months and when the defects have been rectified, the consultant normally issues a Final Certificate. This is evidence that the contract works have been completed and executed in accordance with the contract.

Practical Completion Inspection

The contractor gives notice that, in his opinion, all the works have been completed and that he wishes to be paid the contract sum including any extras. The consultant or you and the contractor then arrange to inspect the works. This is the first chance to ensure that everything has been completed and executed in accordance with the contract.

Often owners, with the agreement of the contractor, occupy parts of the building before the inspection has been carried out. This can make the inspection difficult and often defects found may have been the result of the use of the premises, for example damage to decorations and broken items. The contractor under these circumstances cannot be expected to rectify such items at his expense.

The consultant normally will inspect the premises going through rooms one by one, checking the roof and external walls and any external works. He will be using a checklist containing the major items:

- floors: level, cracks, finish
- walls: cracks, adhesion of plaster, decoration
- ceilings: cracks, decoration, bowing
- windows: cleanliness, operation, decoration
- doors: operation, ironmongery, decoration
- joinery: joints, scribing, decoration
- electrical equipment: switch and socket plates level and secure, operation, correct lamps
- sanitary installations: clean and complete, operation
- external pavings: laid to falls, ponding, cracks, unevenness.

Special attention will be given to any unfinished work as well as cleanliness. He will be looking specifically at decorations and whether or not fixtures are secure and the appropriate fixings have been used. He will check joinery junctions and the operation of windows and doors including the ironmongery. He will check the operation of sanitary fittings and check the adhesion of wall tiles. He also will want sight of certificates of testing for heating and electrical systems and so on. If you have not employed a consultant, there is no reason why you cannot do this yourself as long as you are methodical and have listed everything in as much detail as possible. It would be surprising if after six months have elapsed you were able to remember all the items unless you have a list to refer to.

Some of the busiest contractors unfortunately may rely on this inspection instead of their own, with the result that the amount of unfinished work and the list of defects are quite considerable. The consultant is then faced with the decision whether or not to accept the building for practical completion. If he does not, then he will arrange a further inspection when he can be assured that the list will have been significantly reduced. If, however, you have already occupied part of the premises or your circumstances demand that you need to, he will have no option but to issue the certificate with a long defects list attached.

OPPOSITE: Certificate of Completion of Making Good Defect. (© RIBA Enterprises)

Certificate of
Completion of

**Making Good
Defects**

Issued by: Ivor Barch Associates
address: Prospects Drive, Thawbridge

MW 98

Employer: Peace Haven Developments Plc
address: Bury Port, Marshville

Job reference: IBA/98/16

Contractor: Weathervain Builders
address: Cheapside, Thawbridge

Certificate no: 1

Issue date: 31 March 2000

Works: Renovations and alterations
situated at: Marine Buildings, Thawbridge

Agreement dated: 9 August 1999

Under the terms of the above-mentioned Agreement,

I/we hereby certify that

the Contractor's obligations to make good any defects, excessive shrinkages
or other faults which have appeared within the defects liability period

have in my/our opinion been discharged on

31 March   20 00

To be signed by or for
the issuer named
above

Signed *Ivor Barch.*

Distribution					
☐ Employer	☐ Structural Engineer	☐ Planning Supervisor	☐		
☐ Contractor	☐ M&E Consultant	☐	☐		
☐ Quantity Surveyor	☐ Clerk of Works	☐	☐ File		

F807C for MW 98

© RIBA Publications 1999

At practical completion, the contractor is released from his obligation to insure the works. It now becomes your responsibility to obtain cover or extend your contract insurance.

Defects Liability Period

This is the name given to the three- or six-month period after practical completion. It gives the contractor sufficient time to arrange for remedial works to be carried out and to finish items of uncompleted work. The owner of the building during this period will need to keep a careful note of any defects that may have appeared since the practical completion inspection. These are then added to the list at the final inspection, although the contractor should be advised as they occur. This gives him a chance to deal with them during the defects period.

Whilst the heating installation will be subject to the defects liability period, you should agree always that it should include some of the coldest part of the heating season. This is the only real way that you are likely to know of any problems or faults.

If there are any items with manufacturers' guarantees, then these will probably run outside the defects period. However, you should remember that if some are items needing regular servicing this has to be carried out in spite of the defects period, otherwise the guarantee could become void.

Defects

What is a defect? A defect is an item or section of work not carried out in accordance with the specification or drawings. It is also an item or section where the quality of the work is below an acceptable standard. A defect can also include damage to an item or section of the work, for example dents, cracks and scratches. The consultant normally will be looking for all such items and considering whether or not they can be rectified effectively. It is sometimes more trouble than it's worth to remedy certain defects, because in so doing this would subject other parts of the completed work to disruption and possible damage.

Some defects are clearly apparent on inspection, but some, known as latent defects, will manifest themselves only after time has elapsed. It is hoped that in the three or six months from practical completion, most will have become apparent, for example the works should have dried out sufficiently to show shrinkage and cracking defects. However, there may be some latent defects that will appear only after a year or two have elapsed. These are dealt with under the contractor's 'continuing responsibilities' clause in the contract, whereby he is responsible for a further six years from completion for defects or faults in the work (other than fair wear and tear) caused by his workers and subcontractors.

Final Completion

An inspection is carried out when the contractor indicates to you or the consultant that all the uncompleted works have been finished and all the defects remedied. This inspection follows the same format as the one carried out at practical completion, checking off the items that have been remedied and completed. A revised list is prepared, taking into account any work still uncompleted, any defects remaining or new ones that have become apparent. The contractor is obliged to attend to these as soon as possible, and when this is done a further inspection is carried out. If everything is in order, the consultant normally issues a *Certificate of Completion of Making Good Defects* to the contractor, which allows him to submit his final account.

When the account has been agreed, a Final Certificate is issued and the final payment made to the contractor within fourteen days. This marks the completion of the contract in practical and legal terms.

Disputes on Site

Disputes are a common occurrence on site and every attempt should be made to resolve them without either party boxing themselves into a corner. Most in the end revolve about money and payments, where one party thinks he should get more and the other thinks he should pay less. In the case where a consultant has been appointed, if the dispute is between you and the contractor the first course open to you is to ask the consultant to mediate on your

OPPOSITE: The Final Certificate. (© RIBA Enterprises)

Final Certificate

MW 98

Issued by: Ivor Barch Associates
address: Prospects Drive, Thawbridge

Employer: Peace Haven Developments Plc
address: Bury Port, Marshville

Serial no: **M**

Job reference: IBA/98/16

Contractor: Weathervain Builders
address: Cheapside, Thawbridge

Date of issue: 11 April 2000

Final date for payment: 25 April 2000

Works: Renovations and alterations
situated at: Marine Buildings, Thawbridge

Agreement dated: 9 August 1999

Original to Employer

This final certificate is issued under the terms of the above-mentioned Agreement.

Contract sum adjusted as necessary .... £   91,956.00

Total amounts previously certified for payment .... £   78,230.00

Amount remaining due to the Contractor .... £   13,726.00

I/We hereby certify the sum of (in words)

All amounts are exclusive of VAT.

Thirteen Thousand Seven Hundred and Twenty Six Pounds

as a **balance due**:

* Delete as appropriate

* to the Contractor from the Employer.

~~* to the Employer from the Contractor.~~

To be signed by or for the issuer named above

Signed *Ivor Barch*

[1] Relevant only if clause B1·1 of the Supplemental Conditions applies. Delete if not applicable.

[1] The Contractor has given notice that the rate of VAT chargeable on the supply of goods and services to which the Agreement relates is 17.5 %

[1]   17.5 % of the amount certified above .... £   2,402.05

[1] Total of balance due and VAT amount (for information) .... £   16,128.05

This is not a Tax Invoice.

F852C for MW 98

© RIBA Publications 1999

155

behalf. If this does not achieve a satisfactory result, then either party can make use of the disputes clause in the contract; there are options to go to adjudication, arbitration or to start court proceedings. The latter is the least favourable as it is costly and time-consuming with no guarantee of success.

Adjudication, which is by far the most popular form of dispute resolution, came into being with the Housing Grants, Construction and Regeneration Act 1996. It has been used since 1998 and is preferred to arbitration as it was designed to deal with construction disputes. Any of the parties to the contract may issue a notice in writing, at any time, to the other party of its intention to refer a dispute within the contract to adjudication.

The major adjudication schemes are run by the Royal Institute of British Architects and the Royal Institution of Chartered Surveyors. The party giving the notice, 'the referring party', can ask one of these bodies to appoint an adjudicator, and an application form is usually submitted along with the notice and non-refundable fee. The body then has seven days in which to appoint a suitable adjudicator.

Once the appointment of the adjudicator has been agreed, a referral notice is sent to him and the other party within the same seven days. The referral notice sets out the referring party's case and it should include all relevant documents in support of the claim. It will also include a request for costs and interest.

The responding party has ten to fourteen days in which to respond to the referral notice. The adjudicator has twenty-eight days from the date of issue of the referral to make a decision, which is communicated to both parties in writing. Most adjudications are decided by written evidence, some with written evidence and a meeting. It is rare for the adjudicator to visit a site.

The adjudicator will make a decision about who will be awarded costs and rule on the date when costs will be paid (usually within twenty-eight days of the decision). You can readily see why it is the preferred route as the whole process from complaint to payment of costs can be achieved in a little over two months. Arbitration is a similar process, but does not have the rigid timetable of adjudication.

CHAPTER 9

Case Studies

A CART BARN AND PIGGERY IN WILTSHIRE

Harry Montresor and Sarah Rogers of the Montresor Partnership knew from the outset that the conversion of the derelict cart barn and adjacent piggery was going to be difficult, being sited in an Area of Outstanding Natural Beauty and adjacent to a number of listed buildings. To make matters worse, there were objections from the Parish Council and local residents.

The main view of the converted cart barn. (Nigel Rigden)

The cart barn prior to conversion. (Montresor Partnership)

The site contained a much-mutilated barn used for storage of agricultural machinery and a disused piggery. It was also designated as agricultural land by the Planning Authority and a previous application had failed. However, after consulting old local maps, it was found actually to be part of the village and thus came into the conservation area and was able to be listed. This made life much easier, as the planning

The main living area. (Nigel Rigden)

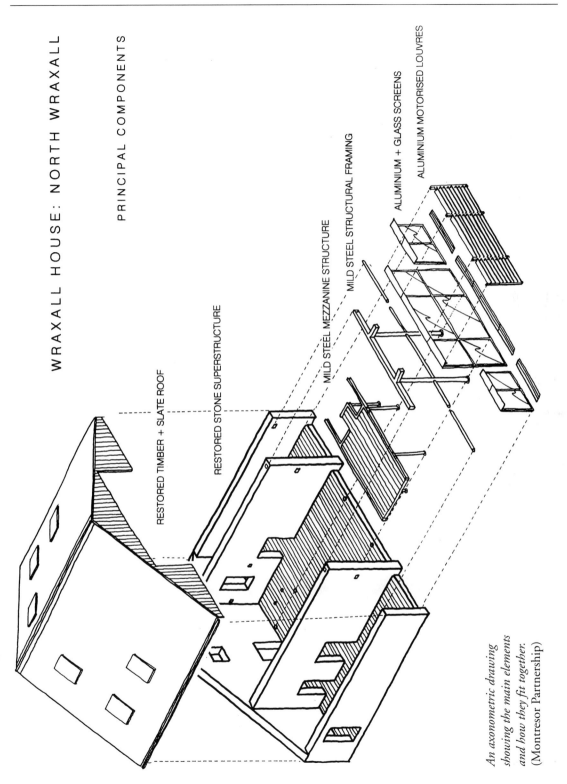

WRAXALL HOUSE: NORTH WRAXALL

PRINCIPAL COMPONENTS

RESTORED TIMBER + SLATE ROOF

RESTORED STONE SUPERSTRUCTURE

MILD STEEL MEZZANINE STRUCTURE

MILD STEEL STRUCTURAL FRAMING

ALUMINIUM + GLASS SCREENS

ALUMINIUM MOTORISED LOUVRES

An axonometric drawing showing the main elements and how they fit together. (Montresor Partnership)

The mezzanine sleeping area. (Nigel Rigden)

process was more straightforward and could be dealt with solely by the local conservation officer. She was most helpful and was instrumental in developing the design with Harry and Sarah so that it would be eventually accepted for Planning (Change of Use) and Listed Building Consent.

The conversion of the barn is an uncompromising blend of new and old. Much of the original barn has been retained, including its high roof space, but a very modern steel and glass window structure and sleeping gallery have literally been bolted on to the original structure. The boldness of design approach has been much praised and won a regional award from the Royal Institute of British Architects.

The new window, which faces due south, maximizes winter solar gain and allows light to stream into the interior. The reflecting pool outside, especially when the sun is shining, also adds sparkle and shimmer to the overall lighting effect. There are motorized aluminium louvres and internal aluminium blinds to control summer solar gain and afford privacy.

The accommodation in the barn comprises a main living area at ground level with a galleried bedroom and adjoining bathroom reached by a spiral staircase. It is flanked on one side by a workroom and on the other by a kitchen-dining area, utility room and shower room.

Whilst the main space is a reminder of a medieval great hall with a musicians' gallery, its plan is more reminiscent of a church with a nave and two side aisles. The south window also makes the space church-like with its height and proportions.

Energy consumption was an important consideration in the design – as it is with all large and high open spaces. The design manages to exploit both active and passive mechanisms to minimize energy consumption. All windows are double-glazed but have *low-E* glass which is coated to further reduce heat loss. The original stone superstructure has been restored and left exposed to exploit its high thermal mass; also high levels of insulation have been achieved in the roof, floor and external walls. A wood-burning stove and an oil-fired boiler supplying hot water to under-floor heating circuits provide the heating.

A view of the mezzanine with the translucent glazed screen below. (Nigel Rigden)

Getting an electricity supply to the barn was an initial hiccup. There was a supply to the village, but it was considered inadequate by the supply company to serve the site. The other alternative was to ask the adjoining farmer for a connection, which would be difficult. If he refused, the last alternative would have been a generator. Harry and Sarah decided to persevere with the supply company because the purchase of the property was dependent upon getting a supply. They were finally successful in this, but had to lay oversize cables to minimize the voltage drop over the distance from the existing main. Drainage was a lot easier, as the village was connected to a mains drainage system below the site. It was simply a matter of digging a long enough trench and laying pipes.

The construction philosophy throughout was to use modern materials, techniques and components to fit simply with the original structure. The prefabricated items, such as the windows, were highly specified and built to a high standard, but still needed careful dimensional coordination to fit within the existing stone walls.

Some of the flanking walls had to be demolished and rebuilt using insulated cavity walling with a natural stone outer skin. The inner walls were repaired and left bare, but have been sealed to prevent dusting. The floors throughout are insulated concrete with natural ash strip flooring. The roof trusses have been retained but needed some repairing and strengthening. As much as possible of the original timber sarking (timber-board underlining) has been retained, although it needed to be supported on new purlins. All the new and old timber was treated in clear preservative. The overall colour effect is of mellow natural timbers blending with the ochre of the stonework and contrasting with the translucent white of the glazed screens and matt black paint finish of the steelwork.

The mezzanine for the bedroom, the spiral staircase and south wall framing were all prefabricated off-site in mild steel and were simply bolted to the floor slab and tied to the existing stone walls. Internal screens and balustrades were constructed from toughened glass panels and new partitions were made from emulsion-painted plasterboard and spray-painted

MDF panelling. A local contractor working with specialist subcontractors and suppliers nominated by Harry and Sarah, who were able to visit the site several times a day, carried out the work.

The piggery conversion was the second phase of construction, being started after occupation of the barn. The building dated from the mid-1940s and was built of rendered brick with metal windows with an asbestos-cement roof. When a closer look was taken at the walls, it was realized that only the back wall was sound. The roof was also in a terrible state and because of its asbestos content could not be repaired. It was decided eventually that the best course of action was to take the building down and start again. It was replaced by a completely modern structure using the original footprint, height and shape. The building now houses a guest bedroom and offices.

Harry and Sarah have given the building a Japanese aesthetic with large glazed panels over-looking a water and gravel margin and suspended timber decking. The external planting, with its collection of rare bamboos, also reflects this feeling.

With its low-pitched glass roof the impression is of light and airiness; the overall colour is grey and white dominated by a grey-painted concrete floor. The building faces due west and benefits from the late

The guest bedroom and office block on the site of the old piggery. (Nigel Rigden)

afternoon sun, though the motorized roof-mounted louvres help to control the amount of solar heat gain.

The underlying soil consists of corn brash, which has the appearance of yellow gravel and is very diffi-cult to work, even requiring a pickaxe to plant shrubs. However, the site has been fully landscaped with grass, shrubs and trees, with an ancient ash tree dominating the south-east corner of the site. A public footpath crosses the western edge of the site; a 'berm' (earth bank) has been made to hide it and provide a physical barrier from the rest of the site.

The entrance lobby of the guest bedroom and office block. (Nigel Rigden)

A NINETEENTH-CENTURY WATERMILL IN SOMERSET

Martin and Lynne Whitfield showed a great deal of nerve, foresight and tenacity when they set about converting a derelict watermill on the River Frome in Somerset. They had already sold up and actually rented the premises, living in 'the shed', the only space with a serviceable roof. Apart from living amid the ruins, they also had to put up with vandalism and lack of running water and drainage.

The Whitfields had been searching for a large enough property in which to live and work, and which was near a local railway station. They found Wallbridge Mills, which was close to the local station and was ideal for their purposes. There were no planning permissions or consents, but they had had several meetings with local planning and conservation officers and the Environment Agency, and were reasonably sure that their conversion plans would win approval. They eventually bought the mill subject to planning permission, but, nevertheless, had spent nearly £40,000 by the time the transaction was finalized!

The site, in fact, contained two mills, a nineteenth-century mill and a seventeenth-century mill, linked by an industrial shed. They had previously been used to grind animal feedstuffs and a great deal of the original machinery was still in place, including the 1908 water turbine driving the machinery that turned the millstones (still retained in the guest bedroom).

The first floor interior as it was with the disused drive wheels and belts. The two millstones can be seen on the floor at the back of the room. (© English Heritage.NMR)

BELOW: The mill buildings prior to conversion. (© English Heritage.NMR)

The main three-storey mill building. (Nigel Rigden)

OPPOSITE: The watermill alongside the River Frome. (Nigel Rigden)

BELOW: The electrical services have been allowed to run on the surface in their galvanized conduits. (Nigel Rigden)

It was decided first to convert the newer three-storey mill, which would house the Whitfields' living quarters and offices, leaving the older mill to be converted at a later date into self-contained accommodation for guests linked to their business.

Whilst negotiations were progressing on purchasing the site, English Heritage became interested and promptly gave the entire site Grade II listed status, which meant that most of the machinery and the iron-framed windows had to be retained. The mill is sited directly alongside the River Frome, at its confluence with the smaller Rodden Brook. A man-made cut diverts water under the building to power the machinery, rejoining the main river further downstream. The turbine, now repaired, spins noiselessly and unseen, submerged in the endless stream of rushing water below one's feet.

The site is totally surrounded by water (on a land-locked island, or 'eyot') and forms part of an acting flood plain. The Environment Agency was obviously extremely concerned about the ever-present risk of flooding to the site and buildings, and insisted that the design take into account the theoretical 100-year

The guest bedroom showing the preserved millstones. (Nigel Rigden)

BELOW: *View of the main living space from the mezzanine bedroom.* (Nigel Rigden)

The mill buildings as completed. (Nigel Rigden)

flood level. It asked, in fact, for a circle of 2m-high posts around the hard-surfaced apron in front of the buildings, to stop cars floating away downstream during a flood! This would have been a visual assault on a listed site, and the local Planning Authority in fact later quashed the condition.

The ground floor of the three-storey building regularly floods and can only be used as a store; any items of value are raised on plinths and holes have been made in the floor to let the water back into the river after a flood. The Agency therefore was insistent that all habitable accommodation was to be limited to the first floor and above in order to avoid risk to human life.

It was clear that such a complex project would require the services of an architect, who could also deal with the detailed negotiations with the planners and English Heritage. The Whitfields chose Nigel Honer, of Bristol architects Bruges Tozer, after local recommendation. They were at once inspired by his understanding and interpretation of what was required in terms of their lifestyle and philosophy. He called in a structural engineer to confirm that the structure was generally sound and aimed to retain most of the original walls and floors. The roofs had been either burnt or vandalized and all had to be replaced with new clay tiles and timberwork.

A planning condition required leaving the original iron-framed, small-paned window frames in place in order to retain the industrial character of the existing building, though new, double-glazed black steel framed windows were placed behind. The original industrial feel has been further maintained by white-washing the internal walls and allowing the electrical services to run on the surface in unpainted galvanized conduits.

The main living accommodation is open plan and situated on the top floor, over which there is a galleried mezzanine bedroom reached by a metal spiral staircase. Below, on the first floor, there is a suite of offices in which the Whitfields carry out their publishing business, along with a self-contained guest bedroom.

The ground floor is primarily used for storage and utility and is where the hot-water storage system and mains services are sited. It also contains the water

The turbine machinery and generator (painted blue). (Nigel Rigden)

turbine and machinery. Let out as offices, the original 'shed' now has a brightly coloured sheet metal roof, which is in stark contrast to the mellow tones of the stone walls and clay roof tiles of the mill, but is very much in keeping with the industrial nature of the site.

The fire regulations proved a hurdle, but while requiring ingenuity to overcome them, they also provided design opportunities. The mill has three storeys and so the means of escape in the event of a fire became crucial and the regulations demanded protected routes from the upper floors to the ground

level. A separate fire-escape stair was impractical, so the main stairway became the only escape route and therefore had to be constructed from non-combustible materials with half-hour fire-resistant self-closing doors leading off to all floors. However, at the top floor space was at a premium and the staircase enclosure would have severely reduced the space available for the living area, kitchen and bathroom. The designers solved the problem by attaching an external timber and glazed 'hanging' staircase rising out of the first floor then popping back into the top floor. Whilst of modern design, this is very reminiscent of the cantilevered timber-clad hoist structures commonly found on mill buildings. The staircase structure also helps to relieve an otherwise bland elevation. It was a relatively costly item to construct but adds to the general appeal of the conversion. However, the fire regulations also had their downside – the kitchen could not form part of the open-plan living area, as it had to be enclosed in a fireproof construction.

The scheme went on to win a top award from the Royal Institute of British Architects under its Regional Design Competition. The building project was tendered and a local contractor was chosen, who carried out the work in approximately eight months. The same contractor returned two years later to transform the 'shed' into a self-contained office.

The Whitfields believe strongly that people should take responsibility for the wider effects of how they live, especially vis-à-vis the way they travel (they do not own a car, using bicycles and public transport instead). They were extremely attracted therefore to the idea of producing electricity by alternative means, so encouraged exploration of the architect's suggestion that it might be possible to renovate the water turbine to produce electricity. This was particularly attractive as there was no mains gas on the site. A hydropower expert was consulted to explore the potential of the existing dilapidated turbine, which sat horizontally in the millrace with a vertical shaft linked to various bits of machinery and gears that turned the grindstones. The consultant carried out flow tests on the stream and concluded there was sufficient water power available to generate electricity, with some to spare. A local millwright – one of only a handful in the country – spent months repairing and renovating the turbine and the associated sluice gates and waterways, which had been unused for more than thirty years. A new generator now sits on top of the main vertical shaft.

Based on their hydropower consultant's calculations, the Whitfields decided to link to the National Grid and sell any spare power. Custom-made

The view of the mill from the patio. (Nigel Rigden)

electrical switchgear and cabling were designed and installed, while the mill tailrace was cleared of some of the silt of thirty years. The investment was in excess of £25,000 and the Whitfields were unsure how much power would be produced. In the event, they use about two-fifths of the kilowatts the river delivers, and the rest is sold to the National Grid. The payback period is estimated at around ten years.

CHRISTCHURCH HOUSE, RODE, SOMERSET

Not many church or chapel conversions can claim to be included in Nikolaus Pevsner's Buildings of England series, in which Christchurch is described as having 'an amazing exterior'. Designed by the eminent Bath architect Henry Goodridge in 1824, this church became redundant in 1995.

The current owner, Andy Hooker, a dealer in string instruments, was looking for a space large enough not only to house and display his wares, but also to use as his home. He had initially approached the Church Commissioners for their Redundant Churches List to see what was available nationally. He first saw the church in the spring of 1995 and

immediately realized its potential and that it would suit his business as well as his living requirements.

A survey was carried out in 1991, which proved reasonable, and the Diocese was then able to seek a realistic purchase price for the property. However, after negotiations had begun a further survey in 1996 reported problems with the roof and west front turrets amounting to over £120,000 worth of urgent repairs.

Planning and Listed Building consent had to be obtained by Bristol architect Richard Pedlar, prior to English Heritage considering any grant aid towards the cost of these repairs. This obviously took time and involved considerable expense in professional fees on the part of the purchaser, who was at some

The external view shows very little change and there is nothing to indicate the church's new use. (Nigel Rigden)

risk, as the property purchase could not be completed until this approval was granted! After protracted negotiations, English Heritage eventually agreed to a 50 per cent grant for the repair work and the purchase price was reduced by the Diocese to a peppercorn figure, enabling the sale to proceed.

The conversion proposals were considered acceptable as they 'demonstrated that the impact on the character of the Grade II* building is to be minimal'. Whilst usage is restricted to a dwelling and workshop, the planning approval also stipulated the parts of the building that could be converted to living accommodation and these excluded the nave, chancel and west gallery. This in effect has left the two side aisles and entrance area (the narthex) wrapping around the central 'atrium' of the existing nave.

The only external openings at ground level are the various doorways and a vestry window. The remaining aisle rooms look into the nave and borrow light from the ten tall Gothic tracery windows above the side arcading and the east and west windows.

Mendip DC, the Diocese of Bath and Wells, the Church Commissioners and English Heritage all had to be satisfied with the conversion and repair proposals. The purchaser took a very great deal of time in dealing with each body, both individually and collectively; it would have been prohibitively expensive to employ an agent to carry out this phase of the negotiations. Part of the conversion process also involved the insertion in a newspaper of a public notice describing the proposed use of the redundant church. Any objectors or other interested parties were invited to respond and only if there were no objections could the Redundancy Scheme be submitted for confirmation by Her Majesty in Council, as head of the Church of England, to grant legal effect to the closure and conversion of the church.

Converting a redundant church should only be undertaken by those possessed with incredible patience, tact, determination and, most importantly, the time and wherewithal to carry it through to a successful conclusion.

Since its completion, Christchurch House has been visited by delegations from the Diocese as an example of how a church can be successfully transformed into a living and work place with minimum intervention to the structure and fabric of the orig-

The nave with aisle rooms leading off. (Nigel Rigden)

inal building. Also groups from various museums have visited it on English Heritage open days. There is an informal agreement to allow reasonable public access as thanks to English Heritage for their grant support.

The Diocese was most concerned that the conversion should not be carried out by a developer or unsympathetic user, as parts of the fabric had to remain in place. For example, in this building the altar is part of the original structure and is not detachable. This and the font remain the property of the Diocese. There was a Deed of Agreement drawn up, with each artefact retained within the structure carefully described and this Deed had to be signed under seal. The pulpit was included in the sale, but the pews were purchased separately and most were subsequently sold.

English Heritage was very careful with regard to expenditure on the grant-aided items of repair. They required Bills of Quantities to be prepared and

The entrance gateway and the south-west steeple beyond. (Nigel Rigden)

English Heritage required details to be prepared by the architect of the new joinery, stone repairs and cleaning. One finial had to be replaced on top of the south-west steeple and eleven lifts of scaffolding were required to reach it. This finial was subsequently blown down in a gale – part of it crashed through the roof of the nave and the remainder landed in the churchyard. Fortunately, insurance paid for its re-erection, but it does emphasize the huge scale of the work required in undertaking repairs to a non-domestic work of architecture of this size.

In the absence of windows to the aisles, permission was granted for installing roof lights in the low slate roofs either side of the nave. These have yet to be installed due to the high cost of the initial essential repairs and conversion work and the limited budget on which the project was undertaken.

The south-west steeple during restoration. (Andy Hooker)

tenders invited for carrying out the work and would only consider grant-aiding specific items such as the lead work to the roof. Their standards of specification are high and therefore only specialist building companies can be considered to carry out these repair works. This is not the type of project for non-specialist building companies and so time and money had to be allocated for a high standard of repair work undertaken to rigid English Heritage standards. Appointing experienced professionals who are used to working with them and to their standards is strongly advised, so that a good relationship exists between all parties and a common approach can be adopted from the outset.

The dining room. (Nigel Rigden)

Externally, not all the churchyard was included in the sale. A strip of land to the north and east was included and the access shared with the grave-yard. There is a Bishop's Direction regarding tomb-stones, monuments and memorials and these also remain the property of the Church. Burials are still occasionally carried out for those families associated with the existing graves in the churchyard. Indeed, to avoid disturbing the graves, the new gas main and sewer had to be trenched under the front entrance pathway.

New buildings cannot be erected outside the church and unsympathetic structures are not allowed, including landscaping, garage or garden store. Vehicular parking was granted, although only after the owner's car had been written off whilst parked in the road outside. This work involved widening the entrance gateway, carefully repositioning a stone post and inserting sections of matching ironwork to increase each of the two gates in width.

The conversion has made a successful transition to living accommodation in the low side aisles whilst leaving the body of the church virtually intact to house the business uses. There is a dramatic change

The office off the nave. (Nigel Rigden)

in scale between the open nave and the intimate dining room, in the old narthex, with its long table made from former pews.

The colours chosen for the interior walls reflect the particular Gothic of the early nineteenth century and help to depict the elegant lines of moulding associated with the nave arcading.

There are only a few uses to which a church of this quality can be successfully converted, and Andy Hooker has displayed sympathy, skills and ability to make the transition from spiritual to secular. The acoustic qualities of the nave are very suitable for potential clients to play the string instruments, which are on sale or being repaired.

A BARN AT SUTTON GREY, WILTSHIRE

The conversion of the barn at Sutton Grey is an ongoing saga. It was first seen by chance by architect and owner, Ed Seymour, in 1990 whilst on a weekend visit to the Cotswolds and purchased soon after. This collection of agricultural buildings, set in 5½ acres, has been steadily converted, extended or sold off to finance future development ever since.

The Seymours started work on the smaller of two barns in 1991 and lived in this one-bedroom conversion for five years until they outgrew it. The recession in 1995 forced the sale of the larger barn and a plot on which they had built a speculative house. This helped to finance an extension to the original small barn, more than doubling its floor area in the process. Although planning policy nationally specifically discourages enlargement of existing barns, the unearthing of a much earlier approval, together with the high standards already achieved in converting Sutton Grey, enabled the proposal to be recommended for approval by the area planning officer.

This is a somewhat rare occurrence and general guidance for prospective purchasers of barns is not to assume that planning permission will be granted for extensions or radical alterations. A building both worthy and capable of being converted is the basic criterion for obtaining planning approval in the first place. It is encouraging to note, however, that if a building is very well designed, then exceptions to policy can be made – in line with *Planning Policy Guidance Note* (*PPG7*) that sets out to encourage high-quality design in the countryside.

In the process of converting and extending the original barn, the Seymours did not attempt a pastiche. They successfully managed instead to echo the character and spirit of the original in the overall shape of the building, retaining and exposing the stone walls and roof structure. The extension was conceived as an 'extrusion' of the existing cross section so that one is not aware of the transition between old and new, either inside or out.

The main barn space formed the living, cooking and eating space, whilst the formerly derelict 'lean-to'

The barn shown in the landscape. (Nigel Rigden)

The barn with extension. (Nigel Rigden)

OPPOSITE: Living space with gallery. (Nigel Rigden)

The kitchen and dining area beyond. (Nigel Rigden)

contained the hall, bathroom and bedroom. The Seymours' daughter Ella had to sleep behind a curtain in the hall until the second phase was completed in 1997. The extension continues the same principle as the original, with bedrooms, utility and shower room in the 'lean-to'. This section is also well below the level of the main barn so that from the outside the long, low roof sits comfortably into the simply landscaped garden, which nearly comes up to window-sill level. By contrast, the terrace and deck are slightly elevated above the garden to take advantage of the long views across the open countryside. The original living space has been extended and now includes a new kitchen and dining space, which is used largely for entertaining.

Above the new kitchen, in the roof void, is a freestanding gallery. This provides study and hobby space, out of sight but not out of contact with the rest of the house. The only connection this structure had with the roof is by providing support for the purlins at either end. This allows the roof lights to provide views out from the gallery, whilst top-lighting the circulation spaces to either side of the new kitchen and stairway below. The strong lines of the exposed rafters lead the eye down the length of the barn, both sides of the gallery emphasizing the original character of the building and the lightness of touch in maintaining its core features.

In choosing materials, the Seymours opted for robustness and quality. At either end of the building,

Ground-floor bedroom. (Nigel Rigden)

The garden room extension. (Nigel Rigden)

they have used heavy oak doors with glazed sections divided by cross bracing, derived from traditional barn doors. These have now weathered to silver grey and complement the natural Cotswold stone masonry of the flanking walls and 'lean-to' gable. The terrace plinth and stone paving also extend this theme beyond the house into the garden.

Internally, the materials have also been carefully chosen to provide a high-quality and durable background, against which to set off the collection of fittings, furniture and artworks. The original oak flooring was carried on into the extended living zone, whilst the kitchen and dining area are in natural Portuguese limestone. This contrasts with the warmth of the roof structure stained to match the original roof timbers. Walls to the extension were plastered and painted white to display their pictures and to maintain the simplicity of the interior scheme.

By using traditional techniques, the building costs were kept relatively low, and fortunately much natural stone was found on the site and used in the construction. Although not minimalists, the Seymours do like to have a home for everything and so they have provided much concealed storage space to great effect. A bank of recessed display shelves for

179

Interior of the garden room. (Nigel Rigden)

artefacts enlivens the route from the kitchen to the living area. These are painted in with the walls whilst the stone floor penetrates under them.

The lower bedroom and bathroom zone to the side of the living accommodation has white painted ceilings of exposed timbers descending to the band of oak windows that run along most of the outside wall including the corner and bathroom. The shower rooms are top-lit to give flexibility of space where there is little wall and a low ceiling. Fittings have been carefully selected, with limestone-tiled duct casings to match the floor and walls.

In 1998, a garden room was added to the side of the kitchen area to give greater contact with the outside and a further flexible living space. It has underfloor heating, a solid 'lean-to' roof and three sides of fully glazed aluminium folding doors. These can be opened on three sides in order to avoid the current wind direction. They were factory-coated and the whole unit was prefabricated in Germany before being erected on site. This now provides a year-round living room to allow the Seymours to take advantage of the best of the weather, whatever the season.

The Seymours are currently adding further bedrooms and living accommodation after five years, so the successful evolution of Sutton Grey continues.

A FORMER BREWERY STORE IN CHISWICK

As conversions go, The Guardship in Chiswick, west London, must be amongst those that have encountered the most difficulty in the building process. This former brewery store and later Sea Scout Hall was virtually rebuilt from the bottom upwards. A cellar, which survived from previous uses going back to 1790, was being used as a junk store when Hugo and Kate Wyhowski first saw and then bought the property in 1998. The idea of a 'warehouse' conversion appealed to them, so it seemed logical to place the living accommodation under a new exposed roof at the top of the house. This is an open-plan room with views out on three sides, giving the whole space a light and airy feel.

An open stairwell leads down to the middle or ground floor, which is at street level, and then continues down to the newly formed basement. Light penetrates into the heart of the building from judiciously positioned roof lights above. The stairwell divides the house in two, with bridges linking the

The view from the street showing the original Georgian features and proportions.
(Nigel Rigden)

Grey painted metal staircase. (Nigel Rigden)

OPPOSITE: Living space under exposed roof trusses. (Nigel Rigden)

Fenced-off external access to basement. (Nigel Rigden)

Stairwell with skylight.
(Nigel Rigden)

two halves and providing the landings for the industrial-style stairway, which was chosen to reflect the utilitarian history of the original building.

Access to the house is across a paved area, which also provides the great benefit of off-street parking.

A light well to the side of this area gives external stair access to the basement. The little yard at this lower level provides bin and bike storage and also a direct means of escape from the basement rooms. There is also a narrow courtyard to the rear of the ground floor which is overlooked by the master bedroom. A thick glazed panel set flush in this yard allows natural light into the workshop studio below. A similar light-well feature in the former coalhole at the front of the property allows additional light into the guest bedroom area. In a landlocked building with a basement, natural light penetration is a difficult problem to overcome. However, in this conversion resourcefulness in using every available feature has allowed light into the heart of the building and successfully overcome the difficulties. So, although landlocked to all but the street frontage, the house has a permeability and openness, which is evident immediately upon opening the front door. All walls

Guest bedroom in cellar. (Nigel Rigden)

are painted white to set off the artworks and reflect light.

Hugo Wyhowski's career in film production has enabled him to become very resourceful in tracing the right product for the desired effect and this project was an ideal vehicle for these skills. Even the film studio's resources were put to good effect, whereby the model-making department produced a simple white card model, which enabled all parties involved readily to understand Hugo and Kate's objectives. Unfortunately, their architect, Robert Sanders, died whilst the project was under construction and so Hugo's responsibilities were increased. An apartment opposite the site by chance became avail-

able to rent whilst the work was being carried out to The Guardship, thereby enabling Hugo to keep a very careful eye on the proceedings both as main contractor and designer.

Before work commenced, the Wyhowski's spent a year living in the house preparing for the project. They were able to hire a good team of subcontractors to carry out the works that not only had to excavate over 300 tonnes of soil and rubble to create the basement floor, but also had to underpin a further metre depth as the top two floors were discovered to be without foundations. The listed façade also had to be retained, and needed to be propped up after the old roof had been removed. All they were then left with

Basement utility spaces.
(Nigel Rigden)

was three and a half walls and the first-floor joists. To link the vaulted cellar to the proposed house above was also a major undertaking. A section of the ground floor and cellar vaulting had to be removed to create the stairwell and the sides infilled with reinforced concrete.

By creating this link the floor area increased by almost a third. This provided space for a large guest room, bathroom, laundry and workshop office. Because of its low floor level, it was necessary to install a pump to raise waste to the street-level main sewer. This also meant that the basement walls and floor had to be tanked to prevent water ingress. The tidal part of the River Thames is at the bottom of the road.

Where the vaulted bedroom is too low at the sides, long thin store areas have been created with access through shaped doors at either end. The same large soft red floor tiles have been used throughout the lower ground floor, allowing the space to flow from one end to the other.

The guest bedroom area can be curtained off from the remainder, but it is otherwise open to the stairwell as part of the secondary means of escape through the back door to the front external steps. Because of the open-plan layout and three floors of living accommodation, Building Control insisted on the installation of a sophisticated mains-operated fire detection, alarm and emergency lighting system.

Likewise, a whole-house ventilation system has been installed, which has helped to keep the basement area completely dry and free from condensation, including the internal bathroom and laundry room. This has also allowed the ground-floor bathrooms to be placed internally; all three bath and shower rooms utilize 'borrowed light' windows opening onto the light well. White glass is used to maintain privacy and give a translucent quality to those rooms internally, whilst reflecting light down the well externally.

The ground floor has the original sandstone flags throughout, although they had to be relaid,

Ground-floor living area. (Nigel Rigden)

thus reflecting the industrial past of the building, as do the first-floor beams that are also retained at ceiling level. The flags lead the eye through the house, to the master bedroom and tiny patio beyond.

The first floor has a light oak floor throughout which has been clear-sealed, and this again reflects the light from the roof lights and gable windows. The kitchen and dining area are to the rear of the room and the living area to the front. Low, plastered balustrade walls flank the stairwell, but do not inter-rupt the flow of space. The stair bridge consists of industrial steel flooring to match the treads and half-landings.

There are two major features that dominate the living area. The first is the green oak roof trusses, sourced and traditionally handmade in Sussex. These are finished in Danish oil, which allows the grain and texture of the wood to be revealed whilst maintaining a warm honey colour. The second are the three very well made large roof lights that flood the top floor with light. These are remotely controlled to provide

Kitchen with living area beyond. (Nigel Rigden)

essential ventilation on warm days. Supplied by a conservatory company in Surrey, they are made of white-stained hardwood with high-insulation 'k' glass. Blinds are unusually housed at the bottom and remotely pulled up when required. A large clear fish tank divides the kitchen units from the stairwell, which required additional structural steel to support its weight.

The conversion is highly sophisticated technically and much planning went into the services installation. For instance, to achieve unobtrusive wiring the first-fix cabling installation was threaded through the hollow concrete blocks. Lighting to the lower floors is low voltage recessed in the ceilings, whereas the living area has low voltage cabling and halogen uplighters fixed to the oak trusses.

Although the project overran the original budget, savings were made by the fact that the Wyhowskis ran the job themselves. They had, however, both already completed a successful refurbishment project in London, and Hugo's career in film-making enabled him to undertake the very complicated task of the conversion of The Guardship with some confidence. The great success of this project is that the resulting home seems very naturally comfortable, with a logical layout and great attention to detail, which belies the struggle the proud owners went through to achieve it.

Index